First published in 2012 by Motorbooks, an imprint of MBI Publishing Company, 400 First Avenue North, Suite 300, Minneapolis, MN 55401 USA

© 2012 Motorbooks

Text © 2012 Tom Cotter and Ken Gross
Photography © 2012 Michael Alan Ross (except where noted)

The information in this book is true and complete to the best of our knowledge. All recommendations are made without any guarantee on the part of the author or Publisher, who also disclaims any liability incurred in connection with the use of this data or specific details.

We recognize, further, that some words, model names, and designations mentioned herein are the property of the trademark holder. We use them for identification purposes only. This is not an official publication.

Motorbooks titles are also available at discounts in bulk quantity for industrial or sales-promotional use. For details write to Special Sales Manager at MBI Publishing Company, 400 First Avenue North, Suite 300, Minneapolis, MN 55401 USA.

To find out more about our books, visit us online at www.motorbooks.com.

ISBN-13: 978-0-7603-4249-7

Editor: Zack Miller
Design Manager: James Kegley
Designed by: Karl Laun
Layout by: John Sticha

Printed in China

10 9 8 7 6 5 4 3 2 1

ROCKIN' GARAGES

FEATURING

BILLY JOEL, KEITH URBAN, BRIAN JOHNSON, NICK MASON, KENNY WAYNE SHEPHERD, SAMMY HAGAR, AND MORE
FOREWORD BY BILLY F GIBBONS

TOM COTTER AND KEN GROSS
PHOTOGRAPHY BY MICHAEL ALAN ROSS

motorbooks

CONTENTS

FUEL INJECTED

COLLECTORS AND CRUISERS

FOREWORD

BILLY F GIBBONS, ZZ TOP

"Drive she said…!" And, so he did. And with the display of rockin' rides found in the pages here, we say, "So do we…!"

This is a focused work of working machines in a cool range of expressions from the exotic to neurotic, and they are fine, fine, fine. Coast to Coast and Border to Border, ain't no place left behind. And one man who knows, scavenging the in and outback, is the enigmatic man of mystery, Mr. "KG," and the unstoppable other, the elusive Mr. "C," who spares no expense in showcasing this array of iron seen through the glass lens of Michael Alan Ross from an illustrious cast of characters, indeed.

It's no secret what these whirlwind soundscaping wheelmen have delivered on both stage and screen, and to the delight of many, they now step out fronting the fierce fuelers for the not-so-faint of heart. Read 'em and weep…! 'Coz these masses of mad metal don't just come 'round easy. These are their works, representing the hard days and nights of sweet sweat to set toward the boulevard where A meets B and back. Tuff stuff…!

If there was a think-meter made for brainstorming, it would make for a gutterful of sprockets and springs… just won't think that much…! These examples of panel-beating art bend the matter of mind 'til it's way outta the box.

Rockers are notorious rollers, so roll right on with a faraway horizon comin' on strong, while these pages crack the whip…! Rockin'…!

PREFACE

Think back to high school, if it doesn't pain you too much. When the lunch bell rang, you headed to the cafeteria and surveyed the room to see where your group was sitting.

Table A: The Brains. Kids who got straight As, scholarships, and were voted "Most Likely to Succeed."

Table B: The Jocks. You know, the swaggering guys in letter jackets who made touchdowns and dated cheerleaders.

This book is not about Table A or Table B. It's about, um, Table F: The Gearheads and Rockers. Kids in leather jackets and boots, with grease under their fingernails and a less-than-strict devotion to class attendance. They might have been rowdy or sullen, sometimes even dangerous, and they were definitely not in the mainstream. Table F played loud music and often drove hot cars that burned rubber when they left the school parking lot. Or the drive-in. Or any traffic light. It was all about noise.

Gearheads and rockers were joined by a common "Born to Be Wild" bond. Marginalized by their school community as well as broader society, they sought solace and camaraderie in the garage.

For gearheads, whether into cars or motorcycles, the garage was their temple—a place where offerings were laid upon a sacred altar known to laymen as a "workbench." Engine swaps, rear-end installs, and custom fabrication were performed here, then tested under cover of darkness with little regard for those who prefer to do their sleeping at night.

Rockers also considered the garage a temple, but with a different sonic outcome. For many rock bands, the garage was their first rehearsal studio, their first recording studio, and their first concert hall. Music roared from the garage at decibel levels as sure to garner police attention as a midnight test run of newly installed Hooker headers.

Perhaps not surprisingly, rockers and gearheads were often the same people—the guy who played guitar in a garage band at night worked in a gas station in the afternoon, pumping gas, hot rodding his old Chevelle, or building a chopper.

At many of the concerts you've attended, chances are the guy playing guitar or drums on stage had a bit of grease under his fingernails. This book contains a collection of interviews with rockers who have made it despite that grease. These musicians put in long, hard hours of practice, practice, practice, played in smoky bars for little or no money, and drove all night to get to another gig.

Success came only with considerable work, but it was finally achieved. And guess what? These musicians never lost their passion for the second loves of their lives: cars and bikes.

This book reveals another side of the musical heroes we hear on the radio and pay hard-earned cash to see in concert. As we suspected at the beginning of this project, most of the musicians we interviewed were thrilled to discuss their vehicle interests for a change.

Author Tom Cotter (right) with Aerosmith's Brad Whitford

Personally, this has been the coolest book I have written. Being both a serious car enthusiast and a rock-and-roll fan, I was able to meet and become friends with many of my heroes. As Dean Jeffries, one of my car heroes, would say, "It has been a bitchin' experience."

Photographer Michael Alan Ross and I hung out with AC/DC's Brian Johnson at his home and at the racetrack, I was invited backstage by Pat Simmons of the Doobie Brothers during an outdoor concert in Orlando, and we were invited into J Geils' home restoration shop, where he diligently crafts bolts on a lathe for his Maserati.

It is often said that talented people have talents in more than one area. We found this to be true, because these professional rockers know the inner workings and history of the vehicles they collect.

My co-author Ken Gross will agree: this has also been the toughest book we have written. Getting through the layers of PR people, managers, and agents is hard work. Most people in these positions are employed to say "NO!" on behalf of the artist whenever they are approached for an interview request. And rightfully so—the musicians' hectic lifestyles and travel agendas are demanding, and private time is minimal.

Not surprisingly, nearly every interview in this book was achieved through a personal contact or a friend-of-a-friend who opened the door for us. Many of our attempts to gain access to the stars through traditional means (agents and managers) were denied.

The artists' touring schedules also made it difficult to schedule interviews. AC/DC was on a two-year, worldwide tour, and when we first started this book, it was questionable whether we would be able to even meet their vocalist, Brian Johnson. Some rockers simply were unavailable to be interviewed.

Others requested they not be included in the book for personal reasons. If your favorite rock-and-roll gearhead is not in the book, you can believe we made our best attempt to talk to them but, for one reason or another, were unable to connect.

Interestingly, once we finally met with each artist in his garage, surrounded by his vehicular treasures, we were like old friends. Car guys all speak the same language.

Now go out and make some noise.

—Tom Cotter

TOP: Ross and Cotter with Billy Joel
LEFT: Photographer Michael Alan Ross and Michael Anthony

When Tom Cotter asked me to help with a book on rock musicians who are car enthusiasts, I thought it was a great idea. My uncle ran a jazz nightclub, and I worked there when I was a kid. My son Chris Barron is the lead singer of the triple-platinum award-winning rock group "Spin Doctors." I've had the privilege of knowing a lot of musicians. And I've met a few rockers who were serious car guys. So I thought it would be easy. As Tom pointed out, it wasn't.

But there were great moments, like visiting Jesse James' Austin Speed Shop and photographer Michael Alan Ross and me scarfing down killer barbecue with Jimmie Vaughan and Cory Moore at Whole Foods Market (it's the best) in Austin, Texas. Talking with Mick Fleetwood about his little Austin 7, a car he's owned for decades, was very special.

Now that we've passed the artist's various gatekeepers and the book is in your hands, we hope you'll see some of your favorite musicians from another point of view. They're true car guys. For most of them, buying a cool car or motorcycle was the first thing they wanted to do when they hit it big.

And it's still a passion. We hope we've captured that enthusiasm in their words and in Michael Alan Ross' photographs.

—Ken Gross

Ken Gross (left) with Jimmie Vaughn

ACKNOWLEDGMENTS

No book is possible without the help of lots of friends. Gaining access to musicians is tough work, and we relied on lots of people to open doors for us. Thank you so much for helping us with our interviews. We truly couldn't have done it without you. If you helped and your name is not included, please excuse us.

Brian Barr; Dick Boak, Martin Guitars; Pete Chapouris, SoCal; Mark Coughlin; Rick Deneau; David Donohue; Kevin "Dugie" Dugan; Rick Dore; Brad and Charlotte Fanshaw, Ken Fengler; Kristin Forbes; Ricardo Frazer; Andy Funk, KTR; Bob Gallo; Rob Gibby; Martyn Goddard; Carol Goll; Tom Grabowski; Bob Gritzinger, *AutoWeek*; Mari Groller, Martin Guitars; Paul Grushkin, *Rockin' Down the Highway* author; Annie Guthrie; McKeel Hagerty; Tom Hardy; Roger Hart, *AutoWeek*; Dave Hinton, Predator Racing; Somer Hooker; Keisha Johnson; Buzz Kanter, *American Iron Magazine*; Jay Leno, *Tonight Show*; Judy Marchione; Bob Merlis; Zack Miller; Cory Moore; Andrew Murray; Peter Nicholson, Rolex; Pat O'Connor; Mick Pallardy, Porsche Cars NA; Brad Phillips; Ed and Ellie Prezel; Alex Puls, 20th Century Cycles; Renata Ravina; Kimatni Rawlins; Gary Richards; Brandon Salls; Marty Schorr; Ralph Sheheen; Dia Simms; Cristine Sommer-Simmons; Brad Spear, Donovan Motorcars; Tim Suddard, *Classic/Grassroots Motorsports*; Pam Wertheimer

INTRODUCTION:
NOISE, BEAUTIFUL NOISE

Rachel Bolan, founder and bass guitarist for the group Skid Row, perhaps said it best when asked why so many rock-and-roll musicians are gearheads: "I think it's the same reckless-abandon mentality. There are so many similarities between going out on a track and stepping onto a stage."

Bolan gets the same adrenaline rush from both activities. His heart is pumping, his mind is focused, and his hands are ready to do what they are good at, either playing guitar or steering into a turn.

"You're sitting there in staging, waiting to go out on the track," he explained. "It's the same feeling as waiting in the hallway when you're ready to go out on stage. It's the same feeling as when the green flag falls."

Bolan has it figured out. For him, the racetrack is a stage, the car is his instrument, and the noise is his music. It's just another performance.

Dr. Martin Jack Rosenblum really likes Bolan's self-analysis. "It's a very elegant definition," he said. "From a personal perspective, he is absolutely correct. It's an adrenaline rush.

"When you turn to face the audience, the first note you hit on your guitar is like the green flag falling at the start of a race."

Dr. Rosenblum comes to his conclusion from several perspectives. His official title is Professor of Music History and Literature, Peck School of the Arts, Music Department, University of Wisconsin–Milwaukee; Rounder Records Recording Artist; and Gibson Guitar Artist Endorsee.

That's a lengthy title, but when you boil it all down, Rosenblum is a doctor of rock and roll. He teaches the only rock-and-roll history courses in the United States to some 1,600 students per year who will be future musicians, music critics, musicologists, professors, or historians. Plus, he's a performing musician and a Triumph motorcycle freak (he admits he has oil stains on his dining room floor).

He gets it!

When asked why so many rock and roll artists are into cars and motorcycles, Rosenblum has an immediate explanation.

"Both rock music and cars are considered Low Culture," he said. "Basically, both attract greasers. Musicians of an era and hot rodders both wore black leather jackets.

"In the 1950s, rockabilly music was played between stock car heats, demolition derbies, and dirt track motorcycle events. It has to do with an outlaw culture, being an outsider, and not being accepted by the mainstream because of involvement in hot rods, drag racing, or rock and roll.

"Of course, when you are an outlaw and own a motor vehicle— what has become a status symbol for the middle class—what do you want to do with it?" he asks. "You want to screw it up!"

Rosenblum contrasts the Low Culture ethos with High Culture. It's not necessarily an economic dividing line and has more to do with how a person perceives himself.

Arlo Guthrie's Mercedes has the best sound in car stereo.

And Arlo Guthrie knows sound.

Arlo says it's like having his friends playing right there in his car.

That's because Craig Powerplay has three times the power of conventional car stereo. And more power means clearer sound with less distortion at all listening levels. There are six cassette or 8-track models to choose from.

You'll know great sound too when you hear Arlo's latest, Patriot's Dream, on Craig Powerplay.

For more information write Craig Corp., 921 West Artesia Blvd., Compton, Calif 90220

CRAIG POWERPLAY

"The aspiration of being on the football team, the aspiration of being a cheerleader. These people were listening to Pat Boone as opposed to Little Richard."

Rosenblum believes the first musical reference to cars in an authentic sense was in bluesman Robert Johnson's "Terraplane Blues."

"It's the 1930s, and he's singing about a freakin' car"—a Hudson Terraplane. In the lyrics, he's talking about this car that is going to take him out of this world. And it's going to get him the girl too.

"Robert Johnson went on to influence every British guitar player, from Eric Clapton to Jimmy Page. And we already know that Clapton is a gearhead."

However, Rosenblum draws a line between rock-and-roll musicians/ gearheads and musicians who simply sing about cars.

"The Beach Boys and Jan and Dean sang about cars, but they didn't have the authentic content to discuss it culturally," he explained. "They were just there, singing pop music, and whether it was surfing or cars, they just sang what would sell."

The year 1965 was the year popular music changed, according to Rosenblum. It was the year Bob Dylan released the literary narrative as song.

"Song lyrics before 1965 and after 1965 are different," contends Rosenblum. "Before *Highway 61 Revisited* [on the cover of which Dylan wore a Triumph Motorcycles T-shirt], musical lyrics had no literal aspect to them. Afterwards, Dylan changed the narrative, which changed the [lyrical] content of everybody afterwards, including the Beatles."

Dr. Rosenblum contrasts the Beach Boys' singing a love song to a Chevy ("she's real fine my 409") to these lyrics from Bruce Springsteen's "Born to Run": "Just wrap your legs round these velvet rims and strap your hands across my engines."

"Springsteen takes a much more literary approach to the subject matter," he explains. "He uses more sophisticated lyrics."

According to Rosenblum, musicians who dig cars fall into a certain older-age category. The 800 students he teaches each semester have no interest in cars or motorcycles.

"None of them give a rip about motorcycles or powerful American cars," he laments. "For them, it's all about bicycles. At the most, they'll bolt on a new piece of plastic to their Honda Civic.

"These days, you push a button on your iPod, and the music is there. You pop a new chip in your car's electrical box, and it goes faster."

To Rosenblum, the interface with the car has become too easy, too antiseptic. No longer is it necessary to get greasy working in the driveway all night to install a new camshaft before the big race the next day. He feels the same about the music-making process. No longer must musicians record and re-record over and over to get a track just right. The hard work in the garage or the studio has been replaced by technology.

Still, cars aren't just a baby-boomer thing. In these pages, for example, you'll find guitarist Kenny Wayne Shepherd, who, at 34, loves cars as much as he loves the blues—a young man with a clear handle on two decades-old modes of expression. You can bet there are many more like him.

Fast cars and rock and roll: the connection remains as strong as ever. Turn the page, and take a quick spin with us. It's going to be cool, fast, and loud!

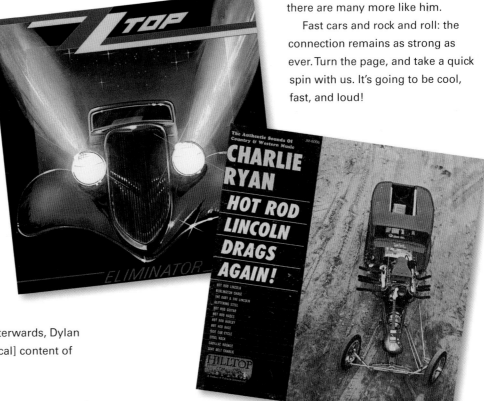

THE NEED

NOISE, SMOKE, VIBRATION—THESE COME WITH THE TERRITORY FOR ROCK-AND-ROLL MUSICIANS EVERY TIME THEY PERFORM. BUT SOME CAN'T GET ENOUGH. YOU'RE ABOUT TO READ A HALF-DOZEN STORIES ABOUT GUYS WHO JUST CAN'T DRIVE 55. THEY WANT THOSE SAME SENSATIONS EVERY TIME THEY STEP ON THE LOUD PEDAL.

FOR SPEED

1

KENNY WAYNE
SHEPHERD

This Dodge is all business. Mopar Performance built the car to Shepherd's specification, and it was revealed at the annual SEMA show in Las Vegas.

OPPOSITE: In a pose that could have been taken back in the muscle-car era, Shepherd stands next to his 1964 Dodge 330 resto-mod. The car features a roll cage and an aluminum 426 Hemi engine. The North Carolina car was rust-free and originally powered by a Slant-6. His grandfather drove a four-door version of this car when Shepherd's father was a boy.

OLDER THAN HIS DAYS

Kenny Wayne Shepherd lives in a world of paradoxes. The 34-year-old, blond-haired, blue-eyed musical prodigy is a master of the hard-driving rhythm developed by blues musicians decades before he was born. He is the latest of the modern bluesmen—who include the likes of Elvis Presley, Eric Clapton, and Jimmy Page—to have fallen under the spell of the soulful genre.

Shepherd is also passionate about muscle cars, high-horsepower vehicles built some twenty years before he was born. And he can recite in intimate detail the most minute details of his favorite models.

It's a balancing act he has managed his whole life.

"I live and breathe this stuff," he says. "It's almost like a toss-up between my music and my passion for cars. It's neck-and-neck."

(Interestingly, this interview was conducted, appropriately enough, as Shepherd was driving his favorite car, a 1970 Plymouth Duster, from San Diego toward Malibu, California.)

"When I was a kid, I had thousands of Hot Wheels and Matchbox cars," says the Shreveport, Louisiana, native who now lives in California. "Every pocket of my clothes was full of toy cars so I would have something to play with everywhere I went."

He liked Transformers, toy cars that became monster-like robots. In art class, he only drew cars. His favorite television shows had cars as heroes.

"*Smokey and the Bandit, Dukes of Hazzard, Knight Rider,*" he rattles off. "If an automobile played a prominent role, I was drawn to that show."

Like many of his rock-and-roll brethren, when he was finally old enough to drive, his first vehicles were chosen more for utility than excitement. Hauling guitars and amps required a series of S-10 Chevy Blazers and Tahoes.

Shepherd's logo looks as good on the Dodge's hood as it does on a tour poster.

"**The car hauls ass and can still carry three guitar cases and an amp in the trunk when I go to the airport. I want to meet the Mustang or Camaro driver who can do that.**"

Shepherd has been a working stiff since he was a kid, but his guitar mastery put him in the position of signing his first record deal while he was still a high school student.

When his career finally allowed him the luxury of having his equipment hauled to gigs by someone else, he indulged his love for Mercedes-Benz cars. His first was a 1997 CLK 320.

"It was pretty cool," he says. "I was the only guy in my hometown to have a car like that. It had plenty of pep and really great styling. I liked it so much that I traded it on a 1999 just like it."

Four years later, Shepherd bought the newly redesigned SL500, but marriage meant owning a two-seater with no luggage space was out of the question, so the SL had to go.

For the next several years, Shepherd worked his fingers to the bone as he headlined rock and blues concerts around the world. He traveled so much and

Surrounded by his toys. Shepherd emptied his garage to show off his favorite Mopars. The first vintage car he bought, a beautiful resto-rod 1950 Ford Coupe, was in the garage and hidden from view.

Shepherd's mother drove a Plymouth Duster at the time his parents were married. He's long had a soft spot for these cars, so he bought a clapped-out 340 Duster with a spun engine bearing and proceeded to modernize it. He's driven it across the country four times.

As he's motoring down the road in his favorite driver, his 1970 Plymouth Duster, Shepherd has no shortage of audio power. Much of the trunk is consumed by woofers and amps.

for such extended periods that he didn't even own a car. Instead, he was being driven in tour buses, taxis, and limos. But as hard as it would have been for him to stay away from music for any period of time, he had that same longing to be around cars again.

When he recently came off the road, it was time for long-delayed automotive reward. He bought a mean-looking, black 2010 Dodge Challenger SRT8 as his daily driver and began to hot rod it before it even had 400 miles on the odometer.

"I installed a Magnuson Supercharger one day and was pounding it at the track the next day," he says enthusiastically. "I bolted on a Hotchkis Suspension system and lowered the car's center of gravity. The car hauls ass and can still carry three guitar cases and an amp in the trunk when I go to the airport. I want to meet the Mustang or Camaro driver who can do that!"

If his pride begins to show when discussing his daily driver, it positively gushes when he talks of his own vintage automotive designs.

"In the early 2000s, I took a little break from touring to chill out and regroup after traveling almost solid since 1995," recalls Shepherd. "I started buying classic cars, stripping them down, and customizing them. I'm a totally hands-on guy."

RIGHT: Shepherd's collection of effects boxes and pedals make a cool display beneath some of his guitars.

BELOW: Shepherd's Malibu garage houses not only a number of his rides but also a portion of his guitar collection.

Shepherd fully researches the cars he seeks and inspects them before purchase. He said he likes to search for base models—less-desirable, lower-end models with smaller engines—because he doesn't want to destroy a rare model with pedigree just to make a hot rod.

"I design the new looks of my cars before I take them apart," he says. "I am as involved as I can be without being an actual employee at a customizing shop."

MOPAR MADNESS

Shepherd is most enamored with Mopars, a slang name for Chrysler-built cars.

"First off, styling is a huge attraction to me," he explains. "Older Chrysler products look fast standing still. They went out on a limb and took some chances in body design, and I like risk-takers."

He also admires the all-conquering Hemi engines that powered Chrysler products such as the radical Superbird and Daytona to numerous NASCAR victories in the 1960s and 1970s, piloted by drivers like Richard Petty.

This history, some of which occurred fifteen years before he was even born, rolls off Shepherd's tongue as he navigates his 1970 Plymouth Duster through Southern California traffic. Of the seven cars currently in his stable, the Duster is his favorite. It is powered by a 406-cubic-inch crate motor that generates 475 horsepower.

"One of the reasons I built this car was because when my parents met, my mom drove a Duster," he says. "So there are some family ties to the brand that I seek out as well."

Despite its tidy appearance, this is no mere show garage. When he's not touring, Shepherd loves diving in and working on his cars. "I'm absolutely a hands-on guy," he says. "I'm as hands-on as you can get without being an employee of a car restoration shop."

Since finishing the Duster build, he's rolled 30,000 miles in the car. He calls it "Old Faithful." Shepherd did much of the work himself, including installing power-disc brakes at all four corners, air conditioning, touch-screen navigation, and an overdrive transmission.

"And it has the most bad-ass stereo system of any car I have ever heard," he states. "It's the most reliable car I've built so far."

XTREME RIDES

True to his *Dukes of Hazzard* enthusiasm, Shepherd has also built a modern interpretation of the often-replicated General Lee Dodge.

Shepherd says that, as a young kid, he believed he was Bo Duke, and much to his mother's chagrin, he made a habit of sliding across the hood, or jumping through the window to enter the family car.

Called "Xtreme Lee", his 1969 Charger resembles the television version in paint scheme only. His car was introduced at the 2004 SEMA (Specialty Equipment Manufacturer's Association) Show in Las Vegas.

The brilliant orange ride features a dropped suspension, four-wheel disc brakes and a bored out 400-cubic-inch big-block Chrysler engine. The car's build was featured on the *Rides* television program, and the car has appeared in numerous magazines.

Shepherd also owns a 1964 Dodge 330, a project that started out as a Slant-6, North Carolina barn find and has since been transformed into a jaw-dropping resto-mod. It features a full roll cage and is powered by a new Mopar aluminum-block 426 Hemi.

The only non-Chrysler product in his collection is a 1950 Ford Business Coupe. The chopped and channeled

Shepherd calls this General Lee replica his "Xtreme Lee". It was built from a 1969 Charger and features a fuel-injected 440-cubic-inch engine that produces 585 horsepower.

Shepherd's favorite body style of all time is the second-generation B-Body Charger. "It looks fast just sitting still," he says. He built this '72 Charger for a Popular Hot Rodding *magazine story. It's powered by a fuel-injected 392 Hemi backed by a Viper transmission, with a Viper independent rear suspension out back to keep all that power on the ground.*

custom is the first vintage car Shepherd bought after he moved to California, in 2003. It's also the one car in his collection that he did not design and build but instead purchased as-is.

"It's a beautiful car," says Shepherd. "And to be honest with you, that car gets as much attention as any of my cars do. You don't see them every day, and this one has a two-tone paint job."

The car is powered by a 396-cubic-inch Chevy engine, but despite its unique styling and modern drivetrain, Shepherd says he'll probably sell the car in order to add another Mopar to his fleet.

Shepherd is pleased that he has been able to make his two interests coexist so well.

"Over the years, I've melded the two passions of automobiles and music," he says. "I've even written a couple of songs that refer to cars, such as 'Slowride,' on my second record. It was about having a love affair with a hot woman in a smokin' ass car."

He said that most of his car-related songs haven't yet been recorded.

"In preparation for my latest album, I wrote a couple of songs with heavy car themes—one about drag racing and the other about cruising around in a Cadillac

convertible. Not because I'm a big Cadillac guy, but because the Cadillac name just sings real well."

Shepherd says there is a fine line between writing a song about cars and still making it appealing to listeners who are not necessarily into cars.

"I think ZZ Top has done the best job of melding the two passions in song," he says. "Like in 'She Don't Love Me, She Loves My Automobile.' Those guys do a great job of writing car songs and not sounding cheesy or too contrived."

When Shepherd writes a song, he imagines himself driving down the highway with the music cranked.

"There is really something to be said about writing a song that sounds so good that it makes you want to get behind the wheel of your car, crank up the volume, and just head down the highway with the hammer down."

TOP: A late-model wheel and tire and a collection of vintage guitar amps add a bit of funky art to Shepherd's garage.

ABOVE: An automobile toy chest that any enthusiast would envy!

2

MICHAEL
ANTHONY

VAN HALEN, CHICKENFOOT
MAD ANTHONY ON WHEELS

Talented bassist Michael Anthony is very laid back for a guy who survived three iterations of Van Halen. Now he performs with fellow car-crazy Sammy Hagar in Chickenfoot. His interest in cars goes way back.

"My friends were into cars; so were their parents. That's what got me started. When I was in junior high school, a couple of my buddies worked as cleaners at Irwindale Drag Strip. We'd go on Grudge Nights, but we didn't have money, so we had to sneak in. We'd hide in one of my buddy's trucks so they couldn't see us when we came in through the gate.

"My first car was a late '50s Renault Dauphine. My dad bought it for my sister, and she immediately blew the thing up. Dad told me that if I could work on the motor and get it running, I could have it. Of course I got it running.

"The starter was bad, so I used to have to push it. To go to school, I'd roll it out of my driveway, and since the driveway sloped down, I'd jump in and pop the clutch. After school, my buddies would push it to get me started."

Anthony always wanted a black, flamed roadster. The style he decided on was influenced by Boyd Coddington's winning "Boydster" show car, but Michael's a traditionalist. So the windshield frame and posts on his '33 are not laid back and smoothed out, and there's a neat-looking lift-off top. He calls it the "Fire Roadster." You can see why.

SCRATCHING THE HOT ROD ITCH

Viewed head-on, Mike's flamed '33 shows off its slick independent front suspension, custom Boyd wheels, supersized meats, hammered hardtop, and those hot licks. "My cars don't sit around," he insists. "I like to drive 'em."

"I always was interested in hot rods, but I never got into them big time until the early '90s. I was doing a project truck with *Sport Truck* magazine. We were going to turn it into a dually, and we had a problem trying to find an installation kit. Somebody told me to call Brad Fanshaw over at Boyd's [Coddington] for technical help. That's when we first met.

"At the Coddington shop, Brad took me through the finishing room. I looked around, and I said, 'Oh my God!' That was my first real close-up look at any kind of serious hot rods. In one second, I went all the way up to the A list, right to the top of what you could do with a hot rod or an old car. I told Brad, 'I *really* want one of these.' That's when the full-on passion started. Hot rods and rock 'n' roll, they kind of go together.

"I sold that truck—my wife used to call it the 'What truck?' because it took so long to complete. Boyd took it in trade, and we ended up building

my black-with-flames '33 Ford. We called it the 'Fire Roadster.' It was the first of two cars Boyd did for me.

"My quintessential hot rod dream was always a black, flamed roadster. I remember when we designed the car, talking to Chip [Foose] and Brad, and everyone over at Boyd's. They wanted to go more contemporary. Right around the same time, they'd built the first 'Boydster.' I was always a traditionalist, so we split the difference. The windshield frame and posts were more like stock Ford-looking, not laid back and smoothed out. And it had a lift-off top."

Michael is really into hot, spicy food. He markets a line of sizzling hot sauces under the 'Mad Anthony' label. There's a special casting on the '33's rear end housing with the outline of a chili pepper.

"My second Boyd car was a '40 Ford convertible. I had wanted my '33 to be a true no-top roadster. The only reason we built a removable top was because my wife Sue [who shares Michael's car interest] wanted it. She said, 'What if we're driving it and the sun's out or there's wind or whatever?' I wanted a car where we had air conditioning, heat, and all the luxuries. At Boyd's, they'd found this stock '40 Ford somewhere

TOP: The luscious red interior on Anthony's '33 Ford roadster is very inviting. The late Boyd Coddington was a definitive hot rod presence. His smooth and tastefully done rods and customs are fast-appreciating future classics, but Anthony has no plans to sell this baby.

ABOVE: Chili peppers are an underlying theme in everything Michael does. He markets his own line of sizzling hot sauces, and they are not for the faint of tongue. Chevrolet should consider adding this blazing pepper to its high-performance V-8 valve covers. It's got to add horsepower.

in the Midwest. I went over and took a look at it. The body looked really great. I told 'em I wanted that car."

Michael and his trendsetting '40 ragtop were featured on the August 1998 cover of *Rod & Custom*. At first glance, it looks as though not much was done, but when you look closer, the hood has been sectioned 1.5 inches to exaggerate the lowness, the windscreen has been slanted back, the headlights and fenders are molded in, and there's a custom interior with a tilt wheel. Sound hasn't been neglected, of course. There's a high-zoot Pioneer audio system with three power amps. The color is Dupont 'Ragin' Red.' "I built this car taking my wife and daughters into consideration," Michael says, "to make hot rodding a family thing."

LIFE IN THE FAST LANE

"When Sammy (Hagar) joined Van Halen in 1985, I owned one car, a 1980 Porsche 911 Turbo. Then Sammy comes rolling up in this Ferrari 512 Boxer. He's the one who really got me revved up on cars. My collection grew from one car to eleven cars real quick. Sammy furthered my interest in cars in general, not just hot rods. He got me into the exotics."

Today, Michael's Ferrari inventory includes an '84 512 Boxer. "Sammy has one, and I've always loved it. I bought mine after I got the Ferrari vibe." He uses his '99 550 Maranello as a frequent driver." I gotta have one of the contemporaries, so I have a 2010 Ferrari California."

Anthony is an ecumenical collector. "I have a '57 Chevy Nomad wagon I bought at Barrett-Jackson that I just redid. And I've got a '69 Shelby GT500 Mustang convertible. It's really my wife's car. The license plates read 'Shelby Sue.'" Rebuilt by Gateway Classic Mustang in Bourbon, Missouri, it's got a 428 Cobra Jet big-block motor, tuned suspension, and trick wheels from Bonspeed.

"When Brad left Boyd's, he didn't want to get back into anything car-wise [surprising because it's his true forte], so we started a watch company called Bonneville Watches. I partnered up with Brad, and the way it all rolled, we came right back to cars. Now, as his partner in Bonspeed, we're doing forged aluminum wheels, clothing, and hot rod lifestyle products. Brad and I have become good friends. It's great to be around anything that has to do with cars.

ABOVE: Every serious hot rodder needs a '57 Nomad. Chevy's classic two-door wagon makes a great driver, especially when it's lowered a bit, fitted with big hoops, and motivated by a hot-rodded bowtie V-8. Mike's mildly raked, ivory-over-red beauty is just perfect. The trick to Nomads is to leave virtually all the stock trim. The gold "V" on the hood got the axe here, but the rest of this car's factory jewelry is intact, as it should be.

OPPOSITE, BOTTOM RIGHT: Bonspeed is an upscale performance company catering to car enthusiasts where Mike and his partner, Brad Fanshaw, market everything from cool rims and great threads to custom watches. These forged aluminum 10-spokes are bitchin', as are the high-performance, cross-drilled, and ventilated disc brakes by Rad Rods' Troy Trepanier.

Bass virtuoso Michael Anthony has a wide-ranging collection, from sports and muscle cars to hot rods and customs. Big horsepower is an underlying theme. There's quite a contrast between that custom '40 Ford ragtop (a Rod & Custom *cover car) and the sleek Ford GT with its hopped-up 656-bhp engine. For a guy whose first car was a Renault Dauphine, he's come a long way.*

"I've been into Ford GTs since Ford's Le Mans racing days. When I heard they were coming back out, I had to have one. Brad and I did some projects with Ford people, schmoozed them, and I got on the list. Mine is a 2005. We remapped the engine, changed the exhaust, and gave it a little more horsepower (it's been dynoed at 656-bhp). That's one of my favorite cars if I want to go out and just drive fast!

"In the works, I have a '66 Chevelle in bare metal with an Art Morrison chassis. I bought it from Eric Perratt, the owner of Pinky's Rod Shop in Arizona. He didn't have time to complete it. Brad and I had some renderings done. I've talked to Troy Trepanier about it; he's worked on some of my cars. But

Brad and I might make it a Bonspeed project and do it ourselves."

Michael can pitch right in on Hagar's classic song, "I Can't Drive 55." There's a car tune on the first Chickenfoot album (2009) called "Turnin' Left." "It's basically a side about driving fast," Anthony explains. "Sammy always interjects little things that have to do with cars because he's way into it too."

"With my hot rods, I hit a lot of events. I'm not one of these guys who has a huge collection; the cars look great in their garage settings, but they just sit. I never got into the high-dollar show car thing. I keep my cars in good shape. That's why my collection isn't huge, because I do like to drive every one of the cars I own."

Mad Anthony, intent at the wheel, likes to drive all eleven of his cars. He credits fellow Chickenfoot rocker Sammy Hagar with accelerating his auto interests, but he's got his own preferences, and they're biased toward serious rods and resto-mods.

3

BRAD
WHITFORD

The perfect stance with just the right wheels. Whitford had some doubt as to whether his Chevelle was an authentic SS 396, so he didn't feel bad about hot rodding it.

OPPOSITE Brad Whitford may be Aerosmith's lead guitarist, but he is a car guy at heart. He's leaning against one of his favorites, a resto-modded 1967 Chevelle. The big-block car has a six-speed gearbox, updated steering, and disc brakes. "Goes like snot," he says.

AEROSMITH
TOYS IN THE GARAGE

Winding up in the hospital after whacking his head on the door of a Ferrari would have seemed comical if it hadn't been so serious.

Brad Whitford, a lifelong car enthusiast and guitarist for Aerosmith, was test driving a Ferrari California in 2009 when he banged his head as he exited the car. He didn't think anything of it.

Three days later, he was in surgery, fighting for his life.

"I had a subdural hematoma," says Whitford. It didn't seem like he had hit his head that hard, but he suffered from excess blood on the surface of the brain. "There was so much blood inside my skull that it actually started pushing my brain."

Thankfully, Whitford fully recovered after a couple of months in rehab.

Oh, and he didn't buy the Ferrari.

Not that he hadn't already owned one of the Italian sports cars. When Aerosmith started to make money in the mid-1970s, all those years of hard work began to pay off.

"Our lifestyles began to creep up a bit," recalls Whitford. "Each of the guys got their own places to live, and one of the first things I started to buy was better guitars and nicer cars."

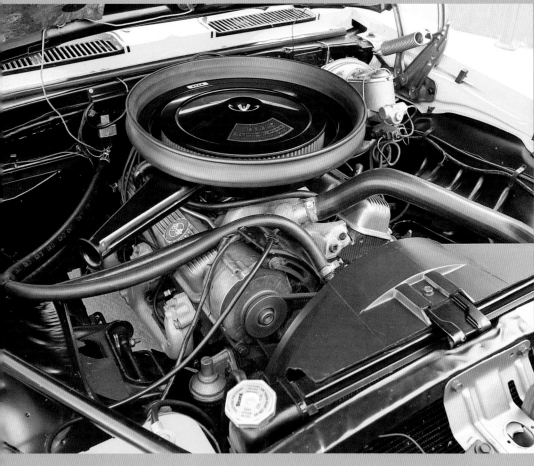

THE DRAGSTER NEXT DOOR

Whitford's car fascination started when he was about eight or nine years old. Growing up in Reading, Massachusetts, the Whitfords' next-door neighbor was a hot rodder.

"My neighbor built dragsters in his garage, which was right underneath my bedroom window. He built things like T-Buckets with little shorty headers on them. He'd finish up a car and fire it up in the driveway and flames would shoot out. I was like, 'WOW!'"

The hook was set.

Whitford's first Ferrari test drive was a 1971 Daytona in Cohasset, Massachusetts, not too far from his hometown of Reading.

"I took it for a ride down the street and was like 'Oh my God.' The sound of the twelve-cylinder just took my breath away." He came back the next day with a cashier's check for $22,000 and drove the car home.

ABOVE: Whitford's longtime companion, his 1973 911T. Purchased for $8,000 as a one-year-old used car, it remains his favorite car.

At a glance, the engine looks stock, but it has been modified with a 2.7-liter displacement, twin-plug heads, and mechanical fuel injection.

"I bought it while Enzo [Ferrari] was still alive and the prices hadn't gone crazy yet."

In 1973, just a year or two before the Ferrari purchase, he bought a pair of Porsches, a 1971 and a 1973. Whitford went to check out the green 1971 911 T that he had seen advertised, but the owner wasn't interested in selling it to just anyone.

"Have you ever driven one of these before?" the previous owner asked an enthusiastic young Whitford.

"'No,' I said. I just told him I loved the shape of the car. He told me he wouldn't sell me the car unless I knew how to drive it. So he took me out a few times and gave me lessons.

"Those older 911s would just snap on you, and he just didn't want me to kill myself. I paid him $5,000 for the car."

While he owned the '71, Whitford bought another 911 T, this one a blue 1973. He gave the 1971 to his father.

"He absolutely loved it," he says. "He would put his little cap on and drive it around, shifting at 3,000 rpm."

His blue 911 was the last year for the T-model, so it came equipped with a number of S accessories ,including S gauges, S brakes, etc. The color was a special order, medium blue metallic. Whitford paid $8,000 for the two-year-old car. A couple of years later, he had the car repainted in the original color at a cost of $16,000.

"When I got the Porsche, it had the stock 135-horsepower engine. I had a 2.7-liter twin-plug engine built for it with mechanical fuel injection, so I probably picked up another 75 or 80 horsepower."

Whitford has a soft spot for this Porsche, as evidenced by over thirty-five years of ownership.

"Now I don't know if I could ever sell it. Or if I did, it would have to be to someone who appreciated it the way I do."

Portrait of the gearhead as a young artist. In the 1970s, as Aerosmith's fame began to soar, Whitford looked the part of a rock-and-roll frontman. His fame allowed him to begin playing with his other passion—cars. He already owned the 1973 Porsche 911T pictured on these pages.
Brad Whitford collection

The only thing left of the original 1969 Chevelle's engine is the block. Everything else is new: aluminum heads, crankshaft, pistons, camshaft, and rods.

In the interceding years, Whitford has owned dozens of cool cars: a 1962 Corvette; a 1965 Corvette; a 1966 427 Corvette purchased from Roy Orbison's widow; two tri-powered 1967 Corvettes, a coupe and a convertible; a couple of Porsche GT3s; two Shelby GT500s; a fleet of motorcycles, including both sport bikes and Harley-Davidsons; and a couple of Vipers.

"We did some music for a Dodge TV commercial, and part of the deal was that each of the guys in the band was to receive a Viper as payment. This was just before the new body style was introduced, so Dodge said we could either get one right away or wait for the new model, which was due in about six months. So I told them I wanted one right away, and that I wanted to order a new one as well. I fully expected to pay for

the second car. It turned out that I got two cars for nothing! I was the only guy in the band that did this. The cars were awesome."

TRACK TIME

Whitford has never raced professionally, but he has participated in a number of racing schools, including Skip Barber, Derek Daly's Driving Academy in Las Vegas, and The Panoz School in Atlanta. He is also a part owner of the renowned F1 Boston go-kart track in Massachusetts. This indoor track rivals anything in Europe, and Whitford said racing there has taught him much about car control. He has even participated on

teams for 12-Hour Enduros.

Whitford also takes some of his current cars to Carolina Motorsport Park in South Carolina for member track days.

"I don't like racing against a bunch of twenty-year-olds, but I think I could enjoy racing in a gentlemen's vintage racing series," he says.

In addition to his 1973 Porsche 911, Whitford's current stable includes a couple of neat muscle cars. One is a 1967 Chevelle. In 1992, he visited Rhode Island to view a guy's Chevelle collection. He narrowed his choice to two cars, a mint-condition white car and a nice maroon car.

"The white car still had the showroom plastic covers on the seats. It was an L-78 big-block car, but it was virtually brand new, with very low miles. What could you do with it? You couldn't drive it."

So he settled on the somewhat less nice maroon car and has never regretted his decision. You see, Whitford is a bit of a hot rodder; he can't leave well enough alone. Whether it's putting a twin-plug engine in his Porsche or modding a Chevelle, he strives to make cars better. In the case of the latter, he installed a modern AGR steering box and a six-speed transmission.

"I turned it into a comfortable, reliable car that goes like snot. It has a nice exhaust roar to it too!"

Whitford is also proud of is his 2007 Saleen Boss 302 Mustang that is signed by Steve Saleen and Parnelli Jones. He bought it from a used-car lot near his Charlotte, North Carolina, home.

Something old, something new. A modern wooden steering wheel dominates a mostly stock Chevelle interior. Whitford kept the original bench seat and dash with, the addition of a tach and accessory gauges. The floor shift connects to a modern six-speed gearbox.

Whitford's car fascination started when he was about eight or nine years old. "My neighbor built dragsters in his garage. He'd finish up a car and fire it up in the driveway and flames would shoot out. I was like, 'WOW!'"

"The guy who bought it new was physically too big to fit in it. It only had a couple of hundred miles on it. So I got a good deal and brought it to a place called ProDyno. The car was rated at 390 horsepower, with about 310 horsepower to the rear wheels.

"Without going too crazy, we installed long-tube headers and a few other things, and now it's pulling about 475 horsepower. And it's a really fun car to drive."

He's owned so many great cars. But is there one that he still craves?

"If someone else were writing the check, I think I'd like a 599 Ferrari or one of the McLaren F1s," he says.

But to prove that it's not all about speed and performance, he mentioned another of his past favorite rides.

"I had a bone-stock 1949 Chevy pickup truck," Whitford says. "First gear was so low you didn't want to use it. The fastest you could go was fifty miles per hour. But it was just so cool."

SIR
MIX-A-LOT

HOOPTIES NO MORE

These days, Anthony Ray, a.k.a. Sir Mix-A-Lot, cruises the streets of Seattle in a 2008 Lamborghini Murcielago.

The car is proof that he has made it.

But it wasn't too many years ago when "Mix" happily cruised those same streets in his 1969 Hooptie, a.k.a. a Buick Electra 225.

"It was my first car, an *Exorcist*-vomit green deuce-and-a-quarter," says the forty-eight-year-old, one-man musical powerhouse. "It had a big dent in it. Hooptie was what we called a raggedy old car back in the day."

Mix wrote a song about his Buick, but these days, his stable includes mostly exotics. He has the Lambo, a 2012 Mercedes CLS, and a deposit on a new Lamborghini Aventador.

"That car is insane, man," he says. "It looks like Batman for sure."

It's fair to say that Mix spends more time in his car than just about anyone else in the music business. He doesn't fly in airplanes and hasn't since 1994. So when he travels from his Seattle home to the East Coast for a concert, he takes a long drive.

"I just got back from a concert in Georgia," he says. "I drove all the way there and came back through Dallas, Santa Fe, and Las Vegas. I drive myself; no tour bus."

The man is a driving fool.

Mix grew up in a household where his mother idolized blues greats like B. B. King, Bo Diddley, Muddy Waters, and Bobby Blue Bland. His father was into jazz—Eddie Harris, Les McCann, and the Crusaders. And his older brother, who

Brought up in a family that cherished both music and cars, forty-eight-year-old Mix has been seriously into collecting and driving exotic cars since he was twenty-five years old.

ABOVE: Mix purchased his 2008 Lamborghini Murcielago LP 640 off eBay sight-unseen. It's the only car he has ever purchased without an in-person tire-kicking session.

Mix says his greatest joy is bringing one of his exotic cars to a cars and coffee–type cruise-in on a Saturday morning, and when kids show an interest, instead of chasing them away, he invites them to sit in his car. There are probably more than a few adults that would appreciate that invitation, as well.

went to school with homeboy Jimi Hendrix, was into Peter Frampton. Little wonder Mix forged a career in the music industry.

Mix, who started as a DJ, now performs, writes, promotes, and produces rap, rock, and jazz.

Mix notes that his older brother had another interest besides rock and roll: cars.

"He was big into muscle cars," recalls Mix. "He had a '69 Road Runner with a 426 Hemi engine in it. It was just rump, rump, rump. The car was a beast. I'd climb into the backseat with my big afro, and he'd drive me to school. By the time I got there, my 'fro was all messed up!

"I've been into cars myself since the mid-1980s, when I was about 25 years old," he says.

After the Hooptie, he bought a Cadillac, but his fascination for America's premier luxury brand was short lived.

"You'd hit a pothole, and you'd wiggle down the road for about fifteen minutes. Then I had the chance to test drive a Mercedes-Benz 6.9 liter sedan, and the

rest is history. I couldn't afford it at the time, but I realized then that I was developing an affection for cars."

Like many of his contemporaries at the time, Mix admired the Ferrari used on the *Miami Vice* television show.

"I produced my first hit in 1987, and I bought my first exotic, a Ferrari Testa Rosa," he says with a loud laugh. "I bought it and didn't even know how to drive a stick shift yet. I didn't have a house either, which tells you how stupid I was."

Since that first Ferrari, at least forty exotics have graced Mix's garage. A Ferrari 348 and 360, a couple of Diablos, an AMG Hammer, several Porsches, BMWs, more Lambos, and more Ferraris. He has owned as many as twelve or fifteen cars at one time, but he has purposely trimmed down the size of his collection.

"I wasn't getting to use them," he explaines. "Also, back in the 1990s, cars had more personality than they have now. A Porsche looked like a

Mix doesn't fly, and because he spends lots of time in his automobiles, they need to be comfortable. His Lambo's interior more than fills the bill

Check out what this Baby's Got out Back! Open the rear hatch of the Lambo, and this 631-horsepower V-12 engine stares back at you. On a perfect Saturday, Mix'll drive the car to an ice cream stand 100 miles away.

Porsche, a Mercedes looked like a Mercedes, but now they all look the same. Except the new Jaguar XJL, which I like a lot."

He is also considering a Rolls-Royce Ghost, but concedes it's hard to spend a quarter-million dollars on a sedan.

FREEDOM BEHIND THE WHEEL

Mix loves his cars not for the impressions they make on people but for the freedom they give him.

"When I drive my car, I don't drive by the beach with the top down and the windows down," says Mix, "I go out onto a lonely road somewhere by myself and tear up the damn road. To me, it's all about the freedom and independence that cars represent. No crowds, no schedules, just me."

Mix is a self-admitted tire-kicker, a tough customer who is not moved by surface impressions.

"I've even driven to Texas to inspect a car," he says. "I look them over, I drive them, I kick the tires. I don't buy something just because it looks cool. Before I buy a car, I take it out and beat the hell out of it."

Currently, he'd like to do some tire-kicking of the new Pagani.

"Not the Zonda, but the Huayra. I saw one down in Monterey around the [Pebble Beach] Concours weekend, and the car is like a piece of jewelry. One of the most beautiful and well-made cars I've seen in my life. But that's more than a million dollars! I'm thinking seriously about a Mercedes-Benz SLR McLaren."

"Half the fun of owning these cars is buying them. It's humbling to own one of these, because I realize how fortunate I am to be able to drive cars that most people can only dream of."

Mix shares his automotive interests with a Cars & Coffee group near Seattle.

"I thought it was going to be a bunch of squares from Microsoft, but these are real car guys who work hard on their cars," he explains. "We meet every Saturday and let kids sit in our cars. I don't tell them to get away. Then, if the weather is nice, we'll drive our Lambos and Astons and Ferraris on a long run. We'll drive a hundred miles just to eat an ice cream cone."

His latest Hooptie certainly beats his original, the "puke-green," 1969 Buick "Deuce-and-a-Quarter" that was the subject of a humorous Sir Mix-A-Lot music video.

5

SAMMY
HAGAR

HE STILL CAN'T DRIVE 55!

Hagar's Aston Martin Vanquish S is an understated car for times when he's wanting to fly a bit under the high-zoot radar. "It's beautiful and as good sounding as anything ever made on the planet," he contends, "but it's a big, heavy, clunky car compared to my Ferrari 599 Fiorano."

OPPOSITE: Sammy wrote "Trans Am" as an ode to the muscle car. Chickenfoot's rockin' single, "Big Foot" is not about a mysterious Alaskan backwoods monster. It's about having a "Big Foot" on the gas. He could have been talking about this ELKO SS El Camino that's been hot rodded with a big-block motor under that custom hood bulge. Randee St. Nicholas

Sammy Hagar, the infamous "Red Rocker," began his serious musical career with the band Montrose. After a successful solo career, he took a star turn as Van Halen's front man, ably filling in for the flamboyant David Lee Roth. After that, he created Cabo Wabo Tequila Company, and now he performs with friend and former Van Halen colleague Michael Anthony, Red Hot Chili Peppers drummer Chad Smith, and ace guitarist Joe "Satch" Satriani in Chickenfoot. Along the way, he opened a successful restaurant in Cabo San Lucas and created and sold a tequila company. This is just a partial resume; the man is as resourceful as he is talented.

Hagar applies the same eclectic tastes and broad talent that make him a musical Renaissance man to his personal passion: collecting and driving cars. Not any specific genre of cars—just cars. Sammy's owned everything cool on wheels, and unlike some collectors who keep their cars mummified in some hermetically sealed vault, Sammy drives those cars and drives them hard. His signature tune, "I Can't Drive 55," is not just a metaphor; it's autobiographical.

"When I was three or four years old, before we had seatbelts, I would stand up on the back seat. My dad would be driving, and he'd ask, 'What kind of car is that?' I'd say, 'That's a '53 Ford.' A little later, he'd be, 'What's that?' And I'd say, '49 Studebaker.' I knew every friggin' car, and it used to drive my dad crazy. We'd play that game all the time.

"Every fall, when the new cars would come out, they'd deliver 'em to our local Ford, Chevy, and Chrysler dealers. So me and my friend would ride our bikes down to the dealerships. We wanted to be the first to see what the new cars looked like. We'd go in the back lot and open the hoods. We're talkin' about seven-, eight-,

TOP: For Sammy Hagar, "Ferraris have the history and the mystique, and Lamborghinis don't." He admires the styling of the newest Lambos, but he thinks they quickly lose their value, whereas Ferraris — like those along the wall— can appreciate over time.

If you're a rock star, Hagar insists, "you want to look special in your friggin' car. And you ain't gonna look special in a Corvette." Sorry 'Vette fans. Better keep working on those guitar riffs. In the meantime, don't try to catch Sammy in this 174-mph Ferrari 365 GTB/4 Daytona.

nine-year-old kids messin' around. And we'd go aw… look at that thing. It's got dual quads on it!

"My first car was a '49 Chevy DeLuxe Fleetline fastback coupe. The [previous owner] had put chrome rims on it, and he'd taken the column shift out and put a Hurst floor shift in it. I got it for my sixteenth birthday because I'd saved $45. My dad and my stepmom put in $100 for it. It actually cost $150.

"I got my first advance from Montrose in 1972. We each got $5,000. At the time, I was driving a beat-up Volkswagen Bug. It was so shot, you couldn't even lift the hood up because it was smashed up in the front. With my check, I bought a friggin' Citroen Deux Cheveaux. It was like a '67 or '68, green with a green interior.

"Everyone thought I was nuts. Why not a Porsche? Why not a Ferrari? Why not a muscle car? I grew up dreamin' about *those* cars, but I'd never *seen* one of these [Citroens], and I had to have it. I thought it was really cool. I drove it all through Montrose.

"I wrote all the songs, so when I got my first royalty check—it was $5,100—I bought a '75 Porsche 911T. I'd bought a $5,000 Porsche with my first $5,100 check,

and then I couldn't even pay my rent. It was like, divorce time!

"My next really special car was a '64 Ferrari 330GT 2+2 that I bought in England, with right-hand drive. It had belonged to Sir Donald Campbell, whose speedboat crashed when he was trying to set the world's speed record on water. His personal car, it was painted 'Bluebird Blue.' I shipped it back to America.

"I've owned so many cars. Now I have a really nice collection. I've bought and sold every muscle car, damn near every Ferrari, every Porsche. . . . I've never been a Lambo guy. I have a 12-cylinder XK-E Jag convertible, black on black.

"My Ferrari 365 GTB/4 Daytona, 512 Boxer, and 275 GTS are the greatest driving cars. They *sound* fabulous! And I have the goofiest Ferrari of anybody. It's a 400i that I bought new in 1984. It's an automatic, black with red interior. I ordered it from the factory, and I still have it. Horrible brakes. Those Ferrari V-12 engines aren't big torque machines, so it's doggy at the low end, but it's great on the highway when you get flying. It handles like a fucking dream for an old

Hagar thinks if you want to be a rock star, not just a musician, you need a car that really stands out . . . or maybe a garage full of them. With a Ford GT, a couple of hot Mustangs, and a lot more, he walks the walk.

car. I don't like old cars so much unless they're like a Ferrari and can go around corners really well. And I have a 599 Fiorano, which I think is the baddest of the newest Ferraris. I like it much better than those little V-8s.

"When I joined Van Halen, I had a 512 Ferrari, a Dino 246GT, the 400i, a 365 GTS, and a Cobra. Every day, I'd drive up in a different car. I think I had an E-Type Jag and the Daytona too. I'd pull up to the studio and people were asking, 'What's he gonna drive today?' Eddie [Van Halen] had a [Lamborghini] Countach at that time. Mikey [Michael Anthony] was driving a Mercedes. He bought my Dino. I kinda turned him on to it."

CARS THAT ROCK

What's the parallel between rock-and-roll musicians and fast cars?

"I think it's two-fold. If you want to be a rock star—not just a musician, but one of the guys who goes beyond that and becomes a rock star—obviously you want attention. You want to be the coolest guy in town on that stage. You want to be the coolest guy in the world, the lead singer in the biggest rock band.

I'm the coolest guy in the world! I'm not saying that about me, but that's one of the things that turns you on. It's having a bunch of girls out there screamin'. It's wanting people to want to dress like you, act like you, be like you. So when you drive up in a friggin' car, you're not gonna go to some secondhand shop and buy the same clothes that everybody walkin' around town's wearing. You either have your clothes custom made or you go buy the highest-end shit. And you want to look special in your friggin' car. And you ain't gonna look special in a Corvette.

"There is one more serious element. When you're on stage and you have all that noise and that excitement . . . you don't know what it's like to walk out into a sold-out arena with people screaming and singing your songs. There's a rush and an edginess and a loudness. It's kind of like the weird fulfillment you only get at 175 mph in a Ferrari with the top down.

"If you become an enthusiast and you start realizing Ferrari's history, it's the mystique of Enzo, how he started and what he did. Ferrari's just got it. Lambo, to me, don't got it. I'm sorry to say that, but it ain't the same car. They don't have the history, and they don't have the mystique. You buy a new one; they're

Ford GTs are very collectable these days. It's a pretty hot ride for a guy who spent his first royalty check on a Citroen 2CV, but hey, you grow.

the baddest-looking machine on the planet. You drive it off the lot, you drive it around for a couple of years, then try to sell it. That tells you the difference between a classic Ferrari and everything else.

"When I bought my 512, I barely could afford it. I was doin' pretty good, but buyin' a car like that was a big luxury. Not as bad as my Porsche when I only had $5,000, but it was that kind of a deal. It meant, Wow, I'm takin' a chance. I hope I don't have to sell it in the next couple of years. With rock stars, you never know when your career's over.

"My song 'Trans Am' was really an ode to the muscle car. With Chickenfoot, the single 'Big Foot' is all about big foot on the gas. It's a driving tune. There's something about music when you're driving in a car . . .

JUST ONE MORE...

"I'm in the head space where I need another toy. I dig the [Bugatti] Veyron; it's far out, but I think it's way too much car. You pull up in one of those, and you're already pegged by most people as an asshole. It screams too much.

"I dig supercars for what they are, and I like to drive the piss out of 'em, but I'm not the rock star anymore who wants to be seen and noticed. I like the more subtle cars. That's why I get in my Daytona or my 275 GTS and people say, 'What a cute little car,' and I say, 'Thank you. It's only worth $750,000!'

"You can only have so many. I don't like to have a

Although he doesn't consider himself a Jaguar guy, Sammy has owned quite a few of them. He still has a black-on-black XK-E V-12 convertible. "E-Type Jag's are cool," he concludes.
Randee St. Nicholas

"I CAN'T DRIVE 55"

"I went to Europe on vacation, and when I came home, they had changed the speed limit from 65 miles per hour down to 55. I was gone for six weeks. I went to Africa. On the way back, I flew from Kenya to London, which was a long, horrible flight. I changed planes, got on another plane, and I flew to New York and went through customs again, and then I had to take a shuttle to Albany because I had a Lake Placid home, a log cabin. I was gonna chill out in my house. So it was twenty-four hours of travel by the time I got my rental car. And it was 2 a.m. in Albany, New York. I got pulled over while I was driving on a four-lane highway, not another car in sight, going 62 miles per hour. I said 'Man, I was just goin' 62. I'm not gonna lie to you. I'm telling you the truth.'

"And he said, 'We give tickets for 62 around here, sir.' He wrote me a ticket.

"I looked at my wife at that time, and I said, 'I can't drive 55.' They'd changed the limit on me.

"And when I said that, the whole friggin' song came in my head. I got back in the car. By the time he wrote me the ticket, I was smiling, saying, 'Thank you, sir.'

"I drove to my house in Lake Placid. I took a little tiny tape recorder, and I just wrote that song. *Bang*, it came out of me. It's almost like I had to learn it from my head. I already had it written. It was a very, very special moment.

"That song has been very good for me. It's been my biggest solo hit. It's stood the test of time. Today it gets as much airplay and love from licensing things as it ever did, even in 1984, when it first came out.

"It's a friggin' protest song. I *hate* that 55 speed limit."

bunch of cars that just sit around, and I can't drive them. I have some newer cars, like an Aston Martin Vanquish S. Beautiful and as good-sounding as anything ever made on the planet, but it's a big, heavy, clunky car compared to my Ferrari 599 Fiorano.

"I sold Cabo Wabo Tequila Company to Grupo Campari. The owner is a guy named Luca Garavoglia, who's a very powerful guy in Europe, especially in Italy. He happens to be on the board of directors for Fiat. I called Luca when I wanted my 599, when they were hard to get—a three-year wait—and I got it in three months, with a special paint job, and at sticker price.

"So I asked him to talk to [Ferrari chairman] Luca Montezemolo and ask if he could help me find an Enzo that's a perfect car, or could he *make* me one? Let's ask for the moon here. 'No they can't. But if Sammy wants our next Enzo, which we don't even have a name for yet, we'll put him at the top of the list.' So I'm on the list for the next year.

"In the meantime, I think I'm gonna buy a Lotus Elise."

Hagar's Aston Martin Vanquish S is an understated car for times when he's wanting to fly a bit under the high-zoot radar. "It's beautiful and as good sounding as anything ever made on the planet," he contends, "but it's a big, heavy, clunky car compared to my Ferrari 599 Fiorano."

OPPOSITE LEFT: When a guy's nickname (and his autobiography title) are both "Red," having a smokin' hot, Jack Roush–modified Mustang on hand goes without saying. Sammy keeps all his rides charged and ready to roll. The only problem is deciding which of these great cars to drive. OPPOSITE RIGHT: Whether it's a prancing horse on a Ferrari, or a proud horse's head on this Roush-powered Mustang, Hagar's into serious horsepower.

"Custom-built for Sammy Hagar," proclaims a special plaque on Hagar's Ferrari 599. Hagar's done business with Luca Garavoglia, chairman of Gruppo Campari. Garavoglia told Luca di Montezemolo, Ferrari S.p.A. Chairman, that Sammy wanted to buy the Enzo's successor. Not surprisingly, he's on the list.

"You don't know what it's like to walk out into a sold-out arena with people screaming and singing your songs. There's a rush and an edginess and a loudness. It's kind of like the weird fulfillment you only get at 175 mph in a Ferrari with the top down."

"My Ferrari 365 GTB/4 Daytona, 512 Boxer, and 275 GTS are the greatest driving cars," says Hagar. "They sound fabulous! And I have a 599 Fiorano, which I think is the baddest of the newest Ferraris. I like it much better than those little V-8s." Bryan Adams

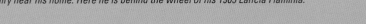

6

J GEILS

J GEILS BAND
CHICKS DON'T DIG TRUMPET PLAYERS

How many professional rock and rollers can lay down their guitars after a concert, pick up a wrench, and rebuild a Ferrari V-12 engine?

An unscientific study finds that number to be exactly . . . one.

John Geils, known to rock fans around the world as J Geils, is also known by vintage car mechanics as one of the best.

This unique blending of music and cars began when the young Geils was growing up in New Jersey. Geils' late father, John Sr., was an engineer, which is where his son inherited his analytical mind, and a jazz enthusiast.

"The first music I remember hearing in our house as a kid was Count Basie, Benny Goodman, and Duke Ellington," says Geils, who now lives in Massachusetts. "My father never took me fishing or hunting or to baseball games, but he took me to Dave Brubeck and Louis Armstrong and Maynard Ferguson concerts. And he brought me to sports car rallies and races and classic car meets. His two hobbies made such an impression on me that they became my two vocations."

John Sr. was a serious car enthusiast. In the mid-1950s, he drove a wood-bodied Chrysler Town & Country convertible, a 1937 Mercedes 540K, and a 1937 Lincoln LeBaron roadster. The young Geils accompanied his father to Classic Car Club of America shows and events. His father also became involved in the Sports Car Club of America (SCCA).

Geils is not afraid to drive his cars, pushing them hard. He often attends a weekly cruise-in at an ice cream dairy near his home. Here he is behind the wheel of his 1965 Lancia Flaminia.

ABOVE: Geils' father bought him a used 1958 Austin-Healey Sprite when he was sixteen. The Bugeye whet the youngster's appetite for competitive driving. Geils first autocrossed the car in this blue paint scheme, then later repainted it red. RIGHT: Mementos from his Ferrari-racing days decorate Geils' home garage—finishing medals, vintage racing licenses, and the like. He has an extensive collection of automotive memorabilia dating back to his childhood days, when he attended classic car meets with his father.

"That's when I started to get into sports cars," recalls Geils. "For one reason or another, I was always drawn toward the European stuff. At classic car meets, my father would be looking at the Packards and Lincolns, and I was over looking at the Alfas and Bugattis and Talbot Lagos."

At the same time, music began to play a bigger role in the younger Geils' life. As an eight-year-old kid, he started playing the trumpet and a few years later his dad took him to a Louis Armstrong and the All Stars concert.

"[My reaction was] 'hey, I want to do that,'" he explains. "I played trumpet in my high school's band [author's note: there must have been something in the water—future actress Meryl Streep and racer Walt Hansgen's kids attended the same Bernardsville high school when Geils was there]. Then I started to listen to WRVR radio's blues show and got turned on to Muddy Waters, Howling Wolf, and Lightnin' Hopkins.

That started my whole blues thing."

The parallel interests continued with a young teenage Geils subscribing to two monthly magazines: Road & Track and Downbeat.

He graduated from high school in 1964 and was accepted to Yale, but opted for Boston's Northeastern University as an engineering student because of the region's burgeoning music scene. He played trumpet in the college's band, but halfway through his freshman year, he realized horn players were not all the rage—chicks didn't dig trumpet players!

"I quickly majored in guitar and not going to class," he says. "I totally understood how music worked. I am absolutely a math guy, and I always got As in physics, so I figured out the guitar pretty quickly."

During his second year, Geils dropped out of Northeastern and began playing gigs. His intention was to go to Chicago and hang out with blues musicians. His parents thought otherwise.

"'Go back to school or go into the army!' they told me."

Faced with that choice, he enrolled in Worcester PolyTechnic Institute for the 1966 fall semester. But within two weeks, he'd met fellow musicians Danny Klein (a.k.a. Dr. Funk) and Richard Salwitz (Magic Dick), and the three were quickly spending more time jamming than studying. From this nucleus, the J Geils Blues Band was formed.

During this time, Geils was driving a Mark II Austin-Healey Sprite, having flipped the Bugeye. However, cars took a backseat to music as the band began touring and opening for groups like Black Sabbath.

By 1972, Geils was married, with a VW Squareback (his wife's father was a Pennsylvania VW dealer) in the driveway of a little house in Bedford, Massachusetts.

A year later, the J Geils Band was gaining notoriety

and beginning to make some money. Driving the VW was getting old.

"So I'm starting to think that I can get a ten- or twelve-year-old Ferrari for like $3,000, $4,000, or $5,000," reasons Geils. "I started reading the classified ads in the *New York Times* and *Road & Track*."

He found a red 1960 Ferrari 250 GT SII PF Cabriolet at a dealership on Long Island and bought it for $5,000.

"I had long hair, and I flew down to LaGuardia Airport, took a taxi to the dealership, bought it, and drove it home," he says. "It was cool, but not quite as sporty as I hoped it would be."

Geils was living the dream, working as a rock and roller and driving an Italian exotic. Within six months, he traded the 250 GT plus $7,000 for a Ferrari Lusso *and* an SWB Ferrari California Spyder.

For more than a decade, from 1970 to 1982, The J

Geils was invited to compete in the Toyota Celebrity Race during the 1983 Long Beach Grand Prix. "I thought I was going to win—I really wanted to beat Ted Nugent—but I crashed after Dan Gurney and Parnelli Jones passed me," he said.

ABOVE: This is KTR's showroom in Ayers, Massachusetts. Cars that are stored, restored, or for sale are kept in this clean room away from the workshops. It's a quite successful business these days, and Geils stops by frequently to visit his old employees and check out their new race-prep and restoration inventory. He usually has a car there for some tweaking as well.

One of the fabulous race cars that KTR maintains is the Aston Martin DB4 GT Zagato replica of Herb Wetson's. Instead of paint, this DB4 is finished in polished, raw aluminum. Wetson regularly competes in vintage racing events.

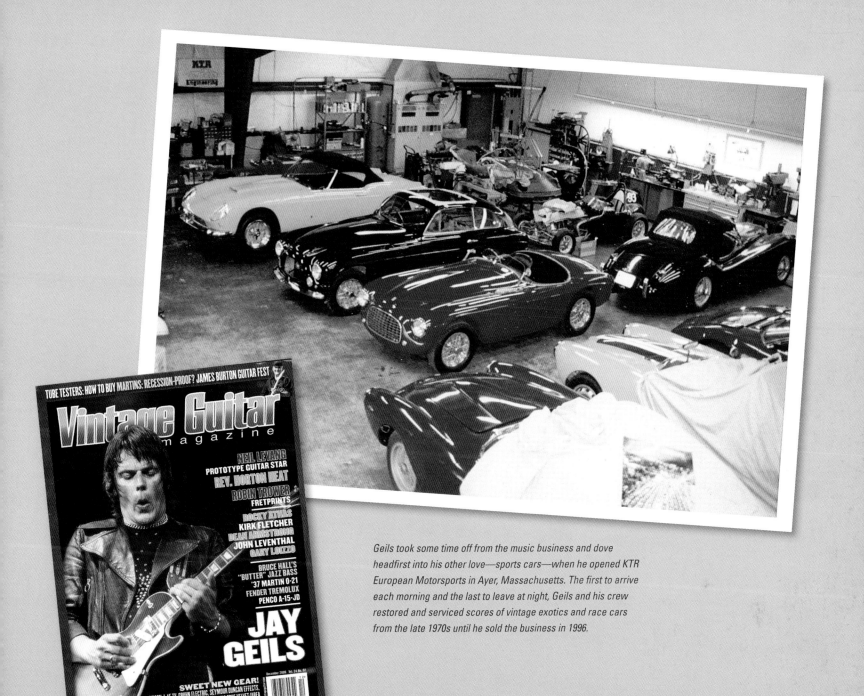

On the magazine cover:

Vintage Guitar magazine

TUBE TESTERS: HOW TO BUY MARTINS: RECESSION-PROOF? JAMES BURTON GUITAR FEST

NEIL LEVANG
PROTOTYPE GUITAR STAR
REV. HORTON HEAT
ROBIN TROWER
FRETPRINTS
ROCKY ATHAS
KIRK FLETCHER
DEAN ARMSTRONG
JOHN LEVENTHAL
GARY LOIZZO
BRUCE HALL'S
"BUTTER" JAZZ BASS
'37 MARTIN 0-21
FENDER TREMOLUX
PENCO A-15-JD

JAY GEILS

SWEET NEW GEAR!
GIBSON J-45 TV, GRUHN ELECTRIC, SEYMOUR DUNCAN EFFECTS,
GROSH ELECTRAJET STANDARD, DIMARZIO TRUE VELVET/AREA
PICKUPS, EMPRESS SUPERDELAY, XOTIC XJ-1T, JANGLEBOX JB2!

Geils took some time off from the music business and dove headfirst into his other love—sports cars—when he opened KTR European Motorsports in Ayer, Massachusetts. The first to arrive each morning and the last to leave at night, Geils and his crew restored and serviced scores of vintage exotics and race cars from the late 1970s until he sold the business in 1996.

Geils Band put out at least one album a year, including the hugely popular *Love Stinks* and *Freeze Frame* titles. All the while, Geils was driving and learning more and more about the various Ferraris he bought and sold. When not touring, he began repairing Ferraris at his second house in Carlisle, Massachusetts, for Boston-area enthusiasts. During this time, he began rebuilding Ferrari's complex V-12 engines.

In addition to Ferraris, he drove other interesting cars during this era, including a 1974 MGB GT ("The only new car I ever bought"), an Alfa Romeo 2000 GTV Bertone Coupe, a TVR 2500 M, a Lotus Elan, an Alfa Romeo Sprint Speciale 1600, and a Lotus Super Seven.

"Because of the deep immersion in music, I really had nothing to do with cars or racing from 1966 until about 1972," says Geils. "From '72 to '84 it was all music and some cars. Then the music died, and it was all cars and no music. From the 1984 until 1992, I had nothing to do with music except listening. I don't think I touched a guitar for six years."

ROCKIN' WRENCH

In the late 1970s, Geils opened a vintage-car restoration shop in Ayer, Massachusetts, called KTR Motorsports (the letters represented the first initials of the mechanics that worked with him). Over the next sixteen years, he restored, repaired, and raced vintage exotic cars.

"I was there every day, the first to arrive and the last to leave," he says. "For a few years, I really enjoyed that lifestyle."

During this hiatus from the music industry, he decided to pursue his lifelong dream of racing a vintage Ferrari. In 1978, he saw an ad for a 1958 Ferrari Competition Berlinetta TdF (Tour de France) located in California.

"It was sitting in the basement of an exotic car dealership in LA," explains Geils. "It looked scruffy, had no mufflers, busted headlight covers, et cetera but it ran. The asking price was $32,000, but by the time I sold my SWB California to get the cash for the purchase the car was in Chicago and the price had increased to $45,000, which I paid after much deliberation.

"I vintage raced it for the next five years at tracks like Lime Rock Park [Connecticut], Watkins Glen [New York], and Road Atlanta [Georgia] for maybe four to five races a season. It had the full competition engine with probably 280 horsepower. Those were five great years, and something I needed to get out of my system."

He sold the vintage racing Ferrari in 1984.

A friend once told Geils that when he reached fifty years of age, he would probably tire of the auto-repair

Dusty but beautiful. Geils owns this 1961 Ferrari GTE 2+2, which he says is the only 3-liter Ferrari he can afford. It rests in the KTR service area awaiting minor repairs.

business. "And he was right," agrees Geils.

So in 1992, he and Magic Dick started a five-piece blues band called Bluestime. By 1995, they were back on the road again, opening for such luminaries as B. B. King.

Eventually he sold KTR to one of his customers, and he was finally in a position to enjoy his dual passions: playing music and playing with cars on his own schedule.

These days, he performs blues and jazz concerts several times a year. In a rock back reunion, he opened for another Boston-area band—Aerosmith—at a sold-out Fenway Park show in the summer of 2010.

And the rest of the time, he fiddles with his cars and motorcycles.

FIVE IS ENOUGH

Geils' desire is to assemble what he calls "a realistic five-car collection" of the five great Italian marques, three of which he already owns. The set would consist of a Ferrari, an Alfa, a Lancia, a Maserati, and a Fiat.

"I own a 1961 Ferrari 250 GTE 2+2, which is the only three-liter Ferrari I could afford," he says. "I have a nice 1958 Alfa Sprint Veloce, which is my street rod. It has a two-liter engine with a five-speed, disc brakes, and wire wheels. And I have a 1965 Lancia Flaminia, which is not a Zagato-bodied car, like I would have preferred, but those have gotten too expensive."

Though he once owned a Maserati 3500 GT, when those prices rose, he sold it. Geils would like another one of those or maybe a Sebring Coupe.

"The problem is the Fiat," he says. "My collection formula consists of five makes, five coach builders, and five different engines—a straight four-cylinder twin cam, a straight six-cylinder twin cam, a V-6 overhead valve, V-8, and V-12. The missing link is an 8V Fiat Zagato, which now sells for stupid money. I had to settle for a Fiat Dino to round out my collection."

He has also applied the same logic to bikes: 1968 Ducati 350 Desmo (single cylinder), 2004 Ducati 1000 Sport Classic (two cylinder), 2002 MV Agusta F4 (four cylinder), and a Benelli Sei (six cylinder).

Geils describes himself as an incurable Italophile, loving all things Italian—food, wine, clothes, shoes, film, and design. "It's a disease," he sighs.

"They do everything with passion and soul just like good blues and jazz."

Geils campaigned this 1958 Tour de France Competition Berlinetta coupe from 1979 to 1984, thus fulfilling a lifelong dream to race a classic, 12-cylinder Ferrari. He raced it at Watkins Glen (New York), Road Atlanta (Georgia), and Bryar (New Hampshire), among others. His most memorable race saw him beat a well-prepared Aston Martin at Connecticut's Lime Rock Park to win first overall.

Alfa Romeo Sprint Veloces are cool to begin with, but add a potent 2.0-liter engine, 5-speed gearbox, disc brakes, and wire wheels, and it becomes a pocket-rocket. This car graces Geils' five-car Italian collection.

"For one reason or another, I was always drawn toward the European stuff. At classic car meets, my father would be looking at the Packards and Lincolns, and I was over looking at the Alfas and Bugattis and Talbot Lagos."

Stacks of jazz history books complement the Ferrari artwork in Geils' home. Having grown up admiring both jazz and blues musicians and Italian exotic cars, Geils lives the life the rest of us only dream of.

Calling his passion for vintage Italian cars "a sickness," Geils' well-equipped home garage includes this very rare and beautifully restored 1965 Lancia Flaminia GT 2.8 3C coupe. To round out his dream collection, he recently purchased a Maserati Sebring Coupe and a Fiat Dino Spyder.

ABOVE: This heavily modified 1983 Benelli SEI 900-cc six-cylinder is the only vehicle that Geils has ever purchased brand new and still owns.

Geils' den is decorated with objects related to his two passions: music and automobiles. Sitting above the fireplace in his well-appointed Massachusetts home is this unique still-life: a huge roller bearing (origin unknown,) Ferrari and Alfa Romeo patches, a Ferrari wrist band, and a tapping die.

On the other side of Geils' den is this amazing collection of guitars and amps. The guitars, from the 1930s to the 1950s, are mostly Gibsons, but also include Epiphones, D'Angelicos, Strombergs, and a Gretsch. The amps are all Gibsons. The room also houses a vintage Slingerland drum set and Mussar vibes.

ROCKIN'

PERFORMING ROCK AND ROLL IS AN ADRENALIN RUSH. BUT SO IS OUT-BRAKING ANOTHER RACER INTO A TURN. ALONG WITH BULLFIGHTING AND MOUNTAIN CLIMBING, AUTO RACING IS A REAL SPORT; THE REST ARE JUST GAMES. MEET FOUR PERFORMERS WHO DON'T FOOL AROUND—THESE GUYS ARE HARD-CORE RACERS.

RACERS

7

BRIAN JOHNSON

AC/DC

HIGHWAY TO HELL? NOT SO MUCH

It's been said that the exhaust sound emanating from a Ferrari V-12 racing engine driven at high rpms sounds like a tearing piece of canvas—a near ear-piercing, high-pitched shriek.

If you've attended an AC/DC concert, you'd undoubtedly agree that Brian Johnson's singing voice has a similar quality.

When he sings "Highway to Hell," his voice might remind those in the audience of a gearhead persuasion of a 1960s-era Ferrari GTO screaming down the Le Mans Mulsanne Straight. It's a sound Johnson tries to simulate when he drives his Ferrari 456 on a high-speed lap through the English countryside near where he grew up.

It's been a long, circuitous route from his hardscrabble beginnings in Great Britain into the driver's seat of that Ferrari, so buckle up.

Johnson's British father worked at the steel mill in the mining village of Dunston in northeast England. His mother, whose maiden name was Deluca, had emigrated from Italy. The family was so poor they couldn't afford a car.

"When I was about nine years old, I'd walk down the street holding me dad's hand, and I was absolutely fixated on motorcars," recalls Johnson. "I'd say, 'Dad, Dad, that's a Jowett Jupiter.' He'd say, 'What?', and I'd say, 'That's the name of the car, Dad, a Jowett Jupiter.'"

Realizing his son was car-crazed, Mr. Johnson went to an automotive scrapyard and bought an old steering wheel, attached it to a stick, and mounted it on young Brian's headboard. "I'd sit in my bedroom and drive it for hours."

Johnson in the pits with the Riley/BMW he drove in the 2012 Rolex 24 at Daytona.

When Johnson sold his first race car, a Lotus Cortina sedan, he traded up to this purpose-built Royale sports racer. It carries the Deluca Racing logo on the rear quarter in memory of his mother, whose maiden name was Deluca.

When he was older, he and his friends would play in abandoned army vehicles that littered the countryside. He'd sit in those trucks moving the gearshift lever and flicking the many buttons.

"There was always a smell about those abandoned vehicles," Johnson says, displaying his sensitivity. "I never could figure out where that smell was coming from until years later. I realized it was the smell of sadness. It's when a vehicle is just dumped because it isn't needed anymore."

As a teenager, the car and music bugs bit the energetic youth all at once.

Johnson and a friend were given a free Morris 8 sedan that they quickly got running by spraying ether in the carburetor—a neat trick until the car burned to the ground. Then his father bought him a beige 1959 Ford Popular, a flathead four-cylinder with a salmon pink interior, for his seventeenth birthday.

"It wasn't exactly a chick magnet," Johnson deadpans.

Johnson was being tugged in two directions at once: toward music by performers like Chuck Berry, Paul Butterfield, and Bob Dylan; and toward auto racing by drivers like Stirling Moss, Jimmy Clark, Graham Hill, and Bruce McLaren.

"I loved seeing pictures of those guys after they climbed out of the cars," Johnson enthuses. "They had those big white eyes, and their faces were covered with brake dust.

"I'd read about them in the newspaper and [hear] a little bit on the BBC. Or we'd buy a racing magazine and pass it around among our friends." He drove with

friends to sports car races at Brands Hatch and the Croft Aerodrome, watching fields of MGs, Sprites, and Minis.

"Fucking boring," he says. "The cars would come past every two-and-a-half minutes. I said, 'Is that it?'"

As the music business picked up in the early 1970s—after having driven a series of crappy Minis and VW Beetles—Johnson bought himself a real car, a Jaguar.

"We had our first hit with the band Geordie," he says, explaining that a Geordie is a person from the Dunston area of England. "I still didn't have much money but had more than I usually did, so I bought an MKII. It was a 3.8 liter, four-speed with overdrive and was painted pearlescent blue with deep-red interior." He eventually sold it to a pub owner, who owns it to this day.

When he joined AC/DC thirty years ago, he bought a Chevy Blazer: "Nobody had ever seen anything like a giant SUV in England before!"

AC/DC became a huge success. Their album *Back in Black* is the second-bestselling record in history, topped only by Michael Jackson's *Thriller*. And the band's two-year, worldwide tour that wrapped in 2010 is the highest-grossing rock tour in history.

It's no surprise, then, that Johnson was finally able to afford to explore his lifelong automotive fantasies. Like his boyhood hero Jimmy Clark, he began racing a vintage Lotus Cortina under the banner Deluca Racing (after his late mother) on American road courses like Road Atlanta in Georgia and Sebring in Florida. Then he bought a couple of UK-built sports racers—a Pilbeam and a Royale—and started to win races.

Home away from home. The Johnsons, Brian and Brenda, don't use a huge motorcoach when they travel to the race track but instead live out of this vintage-inspired Airstream trailer. "Living in the Airstream reminds us of going back in time," says Brenda. "It allows us to live the simple life."

RIGHT: Having reluctantly retired her beloved Bugeye Sprite vintage racer, Brenda Johnson now runs this potent Porsche 914-6 at HSR races. She says that the time she and Brian spend at the racetrack is the one activity they can share as a couple.

BELOW: Johnson certainly gets attention as he tools his behemoth Bentley through the streets of his fashionable Sarasota, Florida, neighborhood. Nicknamed "Thunder Guts," the former race car has a leather-covered body.

His wife of twenty-five years, Brenda, got in on the act as well and began racing a vintage Austin-Healey Bug eye Sprite. Racing had become the family hobby.

Off the track, his street cars became more interesting too. His everyday driver is a Rolls-Royce Phantom, and he has owned several Audis.

But the sight you really can't miss if you're in the Bird Key area of Sarasota, Florida, is Johnson picking up the morning paper in his 1928 Bentley 4.5 Le Mans Vanden Plas, a car Johnson fondly calls "Thunder Guts." Starting the former race car is an exercise in discipline for one of rock and roll's most energetic frontmen.

"First, I turn the ignition switch on, then I turn on the fuel pump," explains Johnson. "Then I must push the magneto in and advance the ignition. I press the gas pedal, which is in the middle of the three foot pedals. Then make sure it is out of gear and hit the starter button. It's not as easy as you would think."

VROOOOM! The huge engine fires up with a deep bass exhaust note, a contrast to Johnson's Ferrari.

Johnson is in amazing physical condition, which is obvious as he commands the steering wheel of the giant Bentley and drives through his neighborhood, past Toyota Camrys and Chevy Suburbans. It's a very manly, very busy car to drive, and he hand signals for turns while simultaneously adjusting the engine's timing.

As we drive along the beautiful Sarasota waterfront in this eighty-year-old behemoth, Johnson casually points to an attractive modern building.

"See that hospital over there?" he asks. "I sponsor the children's ward." Not a brag, just a fact.

After a lap of the town, Johnson returns to his beautiful waterfront home. To shut the car down, he must reverse its complex starting procedure.

With AC/DC's worldwide concert tour behind him, he and Brenda are making up for two years of no racing

Wind in the hair and bugs in the teeth! Preferring to drive his 1928 Bentley 4.5 Le Mans Vaden Plas over his modern cars, Johnson fires up the beast each day to "fetch the morning paper."

ABOVE: Johnson purchased this 300 cc Vespa from a Barnum & Bailey Circus auction. It had been a clown car, and he says, "It's a little bastard, but it works!"

With tongue in cheek and a stiff upper lip, Johnson promotes the title to a classic AC/DC tune on the Vespa's door.

by treating themselves to new race cars. Brian purchased a 1965 Lola T-70 Can-Am racer, a very significant car that left an impression on him when he was about seventeen years old. He acquired it as a basket case and had it restored to like-new condition by Predator Performance. The car retains its rare Ford Hi-Po 289 engine.

"It's got power," he said after taking it on its first few shake-down laps at the 2011 Walter Mitty Challenge race at Road Atlanta. "We're knocking out 610 horsepower. Just unbelievable. When I first jumped in, the power made this a frightening lump of machinery. But now I get it."

Brenda has a Porsche 914-6, which was originally campaigned by the Brumos Racing team of Jacksonville, Florida. She likes what racing does to her husband. "It gives him an outlet, another way to channel his energies," says the former television news anchor and journalist.

"Cars and racing occupy Brian's time, not rock and roll. He loves reading magazines and books about cars and watching racing documentaries on TV."

Racing has allowed the couple to escape the high profile of the entertainment world and disappear into the background at races where fellow competitors treat them like any other racers.

"This is the quiet time in our lives," she says.

With the real "Thunder Guts" parked in the foreground, this wall mural graces the inside of Johnson's garage. It features Brian and his wife, Brenda, racing in an imaginary 24 Hours of Le Mans.

TOP: A quirky car everywhere except, perhaps, in France, Johnson thinks this Citroen DS21 is the most beautiful car ever built.

ABOVE: Four Weber carburetors and tuned exhaust headers on this small-block Ford racing engine help put the power to the pavement in Johnson's vintage Lola T70 Can-Am car. Predator Racing, the race shop that prepares Johnson's cars for the track, restored this racer from a pile of parts.

RIGHT: Fulfilling a lifelong dream to race professionally like his boyhood heroes Stirling Moss and Jimmy Clark, Johnson drove a Riley/BMW in the 2012 Rolex 24 at Daytona. With a play-on-words from the bestselling AC/DC album, his Highway to Help team raced to earn funds for children's charities. Mechanical issues plagued the team, resulting in a 32nd-place finish.

8

JOHN
OATES

HALL & OATES
DEALING WITH DUAL OBSESSIONS

"I bought the first Porsche Turbo Carrera that came out in 1976. It was at Beverly Hills Porsche, and Rod Stewart wanted to buy it. So I sent my manager out there to make sure I got it."

Dressed for business, Oates prepares to go onto the track in his Sports 2000 racer. John Oates collection

In 1985, John Oates had two careers. The whole world knew about one: his band, Hall & Oates, which had just released the studio album *Big Bang Boom* and a concert album, *Live at the Apollo.* Just the year before, Hall & Oates had been named the most successful duo in rock-and-roll history, and they were regularly topping the charts with singles like "Sara Smile," "I Can't Go For That," and "Adult Education."

He had been working quietly on his second, lower profile career for a decade. Oates had slowly worked his way up the auto-racing ranks from go-karts to amateur sports car racing to professional road racing.

But a jammed transmission while racing a factory-backed Pontiac Fiero through Road America's challenging "kink" ended his second career in the blink of an eye.

As a youngster growing up in Philadelphia, Oates was a regular *Road & Track* magazine reader. Through those pages, he began to admire racing legends like Stirling Moss and Tazio Nuvolari. In junior high, a friend's father turned Oates onto MGs and Austin Mini Coopers.

"I had been doing music my whole life," says Oates. "I had been playing with Daryl [Hall], and in the mid-1970s, I finally had a bit of money, which gave me a chance to do some other things I wanted to do. I thought, 'Let me try my hand at racing.'"

Oates bought a go-kart and raced it at a track on Long Island's east-end town of Westhampton. He attended racing schools in Pocono, Pennsylvania, and at England's Brands Hatch. Oates earned his racing license and began racing Formula Fords at tracks like Bridgehampton Race Circuit on Long Island and Lime Rock Park

in Connecticut. Simultaneously, he was building a small car collection.

"We had just finished a gig in Las Vegas [in the late 1970s], and our tour bus passed a 1955 Chevy convertible at a collector car dealership," he says. "It was absolutely beautiful in turquoise and white. It had a Corvette engine and dual exhaust. I bought it on the spot."

Oates' enthusiasm must have been contagious, because another of his band's guitar players bought a 1952 Mercury at the same time and from the same dealer.

The Chevy acquisition then led to a sports car buying spree that included a 1956 Porsche 356 Speedster, a 1967 Austin-Healey 3000, a 1968 Jaguar E-Type, and a 1970 Alfa Romeo Spider.

"I bought the first Porsche Turbo Carrera that came out in 1976," he says. "It was at Beverly Hills Porsche, and Rod Stewart wanted to buy it. So I sent my manager out there to make sure I got it. It was a very serious, vicious car."

Vicious or not, Oates could not leave well enough alone. He had the car modified with a variable turbo boost before driving it cross-country to his home in Connecticut.

While on tour in Europe in the early 1980s, Oates had a private tour of the Porsche factory in Stuttgart, Germany. At the conclusion of the tour, he placed an order for a custom 1984 Porsche 911 Carrera with a one-of-a-kind Pearl White paint job and gray leather interior. "It was an amazing car," he says.

RACING GETS SERIOUS

Through the 1980s, Oates continued to climb the auto-racing ladder. He decided he didn't want to race the fragile Formula Ford open-wheel cars anymore, so he switched to the Sports 2000 class.

"I felt more comfortable racing with a body around me," says Oates. "Plus they were paying prize money

The hair dates the photo. Oates raced in the Sports 2000 series for three years, where he was one of the most competitive drivers. John Oates collection

Oates, sporting his once-famous mustache, waits to climb into his IMSA GTU Pontiac Fiero in the mid-1980s. It was the professional ride he had dreamed of as a kid, but a mechanical failure while racing at Wisconsin's fast Elkhart Lake track ended his driving career. John Oates collection

in the Pro 2000 series, so it gave me the opportunity to race a little more seriously than I had."

Invited to co-drive a Porsche 924 GTR race car with veteran racer George Drolsom at Lime Rock Park, Oates impressed both fans and professional racers alike. He was able to make up a two-lap deficit to put the car in second place.

"It was the first time I had driven a closed car," he says. "When I got out, I almost passed out from heat exhaustion."

That drive got the attention of Pontiac Racing brass. Oates was invited to co-drive a factory-backed Pontiac Fiero in the professional IMSA GTU class with veteran driver Bob Earl. After a few races in the Huffaker Engineering–backed car, the pop star was beginning to get the hang of it.

Then came the terrible wreck at Wisconsin's Road America race course.

"I was driving the first stint, and unfortunately, the transmission locked up," recalls Oates. "The next thing I remember was waking up in the ambulance on the way to the hospital."

The head injuries Oates sustained were enough to convince him to end his professional racing career.

Fortunately, his music career has never hit a similar kink, and Oates continues performing today with Daryl Hall and as a solo act.

These days, his once-impressive car collection is no more. He sold those when he moved to Colorado in the late 1980s. Today, he keeps a low profile in a Toyota 4x4 truck or an Audi A4.

"Colorado is not a great state for exotic cars," he says. "We have a short summer, and there are lots of gravel and dirt roads. It's a rough environment for nice cars."

Still, interesting cars continue to pass through Oates' garage. In 1996, he modified an Audi A4 with aftermarket tuning hardware from Germany, including a big turbo and exhaust system. The car appeared in *Automobile Magazine* and offered performance comparable to the factory's Audi S4. He also recently sold his Mini Cooper with the John Cooper Works package, which he describes as "a handful out here in the winter."

Despite the crash at Road America, he still keeps his hand in racing, although not in full-scale automobiles. Oates has re-discovered go-karts and races at tracks in Denver and Grand Junction, Colorado, when time allows.

Oates' current dream car? An Audi R8.

"I'm an Audi fan and have owned about five or six of them," he enthuses. "They got it going on. There is something about the R8 that is really decent. I like its performance, but at the same time, it looks really comfortable."

And there is the possibility of another small car collection in his future. Oates and his wife recently purchased a second home in Nashville, Tennessee, which has roads much more suited to collector car ownership.

"Without the harsh winters, I can see spending more time there, which would open up a variety of cool cars I could buy," he says.

Maybe starting with a 1956 Porsche Speedster.

"I'm an Audi fan and have owned about five or six of them. They got it going on."

Oates performing in Connecticut. These days, he splits his time between his longtime music partner, Daryl Hall, and his solo career.

9

NICK
MASON

Mason said that he never wanted to be a collector, only a racer. But instead of needing to sell one race car to afford another, he's been fortunate enough to keep just about all of them, as illustrated by this view of his North London garage.

OPPOSITE: Mason's 1935 Aston Martin Ulster LM21 is the first car he ever raced. In fact, all the Masons—wife and children—have raced it. The Ulster is a close second to the GTO among Mason's favorites.

PINK FLOYD DRUMMER
RACING TO THE BEAT
OF HIS OWN DRUM

Nick Mason has written a superb book entitled *Passion for Speed*, in which he highlights twenty-four significant automobiles that, for one reason or another, helped shape the last century's transportation culture.

The 220-plus page coffee-table book is elegantly designed with huge color photos and probably 35,000 words of copy. But it was the nineteen-word dedication in the front of the book that showed me just how passionate and appreciative Mason was for his family and the opportunity to be involved in vintage motorsport:

To my father, Bill Mason, who got me into all this, and to my mother for allowing him to.

Mason is a man rich beyond words in terms of fame, yet he still shows appreciation for his family. He now enjoys the means to play with the full-scale versions of the Matchbox and Dinky Toys cars he admired as a boy. "I was brought up in a very car-friendly environment," says the sixty-seven-year-old Mason, who has been the drummer for Pink Floyd since the band's launch in 1965. Pink Floyd ranks as one of the most successful and popular rock bands of all time, having sold in excess of 200 million albums worldwide.

"My dad's road car was a 1930 4.5-liter Bentley Vanden Plas. He used to race it a bit too." As a seven-year-old, Mason would accompany his father to Bentley Owners Club races at circuits like Silverstone, acting as a pit crew, although "not necessarily a helpful one."

Mason's father was a documentary filmmaker who worked for Shell Oil Company making auto racing movies. Enzo Ferrari once arranged for Bill to drive in the 1953 Mille Miglia with a movie camera mounted on a 166MM Vignale Spyder. The car finished 56th.

Young Mason grew up not fully understanding how significant his family's automotive experiences were, but they were to influence his automotive preferences decades hence.

Mason's own automotive career started rather inauspiciously with a 1927 Austin 7.

"My dad helped find it for me," he says. "We had to do some engineering to make it work. It was a Chummy, which had a bathtub sort of look. When I wanted something more sporty, I bought Nippy, which was a two-seater version. I did some horrible things in that car."

Though his passion for cars evolved first, rock and roll soon captured Mason's attention. His first musical idols were Bill Haley, Chuck Berry, Little Richard, and Fats Domino.

As a thirteen or fourteen year old, Mason and friends formed a band and played for fun, but it didn't stick. Playing music was a youthful fad. He was entering college and had more important things to do.

"Then, almost by mistake, someone wanted music played and asked if anyone at the college might help out," he recalled. "Four of us raised our hands and said yes. Three of the four included Roger [Waters], Rick [Wright], and myself [the three founders of Pink Floyd]. We had no grand plan; it just sort of developed. Other people became interested in what we were playing, and it just developed. I never really saw it as where I would end up."

After Pink Floyd's Dark Side of the Moon album, Mason had the time and the finances to do more vintage racing. Here, he prepares to compete in his Maserati 250F at a VSSC historic race meeting at Silverstone in the early 1980s.

LEFT: Mason considers his GTO "the ultimate, all around car." Only thirty-nine GTOs were manufactured, and because of their rarity and fantastic looks, their prices today read like telephone numbers. This particular car finished third in the 1962 running of the 24 Hours of Le Mans.

BELOW: Mason's favorite car is this Ferrari 250 GTO, serial number 3757. He's driven each of his two daughters to their weddings in it and regularly races it. Even his wife is comfortable driving it! "I've never come across anything better!" he exclaims.

Cars were put on hold while his drumming career developed. In fact, the 1.5-liter Aston Martin International he purchased while in college—with the intention of restoring and vintage racing it—sat at the curb for several years.

Cars became appliances; they came and went according to what was happening with Pink Floyd.

Then *Dark Side of the Moon* hit the charts.

"Then I could afford to go motor racing," says Mason, who, at the time, owned an Aston Martin restoration business with partner Derek Edwards. "Derek said he could always tell when the band was getting ready to tour because I would come into the workshop and strip a car completely of every component, then leave for a year. It would always be his job to put it back together."

Mason is as comfortable twirling wrenches as he is drum sticks.

"I was a very hands-on guy. But racing has gotten so serious, I stopped doing it. I could no longer trust myself. A race mechanic is a bit like an aircraft mechanic; you don't want someone like me who just might have gone to do something else that night and left half the nuts and bolts in the wrong place."

Mason declines to call his group of cars a collection. He feels the word has no passion.

"Competition has always been the driving thing for me," he explains. "I just wanted to go racing. So what I was able to do was, instead of having to sell one race car to buy the next, I ended up with a stable of race cars."

Regardless of how he achieved it, he owns a world-class stable of cars rivaling any serious collection in the world. His garage is eclectic as well, populated with cars as lowly as a Ford Model T and as fearsome as a 650-horsepower Ferrari Enzo.

His oldest car is a 1901 French Panhard. His quickest is likely his 1983 Tyrell 011 Formula One racer. From a 1927 Bugatti to a 1955 Jaguar D-Type to a 1995 McLaren F1 GTR, Mason has one requirement before a car enters his garage—it must be a race car.

"I think I've raced everything I own," he says, but then thought better. "Well, except for that Model T, which must be the most dangerous car ever built."

His favorite? Without hesitation, the 1962 Ferrari GTO he purchased thirty-five years ago for the then insanely high price of 35,000 pounds sterling. With a limited production run of just thirty-six cars, the GTO has become the car of many dreams. These days, when GTOs change hands, which is rarely, the going price is $30 million and more.

"It does so many things well," says Mason enthusiastically. "Recently, I raced it at Goodwood, finishing second in the TT. Then three days later, it was in Italy with my wife on a ladies-only rally. Then it sat outside of Ralph Lauren's shop in London, adding a bit of spice to the evening, and I've driven both my daughters to the church for their weddings in the car. It is the ultimate all-around car. I've never come across anything better."

For Mason, speed is secondary to style. "Speed is something that everyone understood," he says. "People managed to go fast very early on. In 1911, the Blitzen Benz ran at 140 miles per hour.

"Competition has always been the driving thing for me, I just wanted to go racing."

"What's much more interesting is what Adrian Newey [engineer, designer, and aerodynamicist for Red Bull's Formula One program] is doing. It's ultimately form. It was the same with vintage Bugattis—just the simplicity and elegance of the design.

"The Germans brought engineering that approached art to the Silver Arrows Grand Prix teams in the 1930s. And much of today's style is hidden as a black art of down-force and suspension."

For a time, Mason experimented with modern racing's black arts. Even though his passion was for vintage sports cars, he has entered the 24 Hours of Le Mans five times in the past decade.

"It was my dream come true," he says. "Growing up, I never had crazed notions of racing at Indianapolis

For Mason, speed is secondary to style. Here, he races his Bugatti Type 35 at Silverstone in the early 1980s. The Bugatti is attractive to him because of "its simplicity, and its elegance, really."

Mason's office in North London is filled with memorabilia related to his racing and music passions.

or Formula One, but Le Mans seemed to me to be the ultimate glamorous race. When I raced there, it was still a place where an amateur could compete and maybe even finish with a trophy."

When asked what his ultimate car would be, he says that he already owned it: his Ferrari GTO. But pondering a few moments, he revises his answer.

"I think the ultimate car for me is the 1955 Mercedes-Benz SLR that Stirling [Moss] and Denis Jenkins drove to win the Mille," he says. "That car is so unique, so special, and the history is just fantastic."

Mason knows he is a fortunate guy.

"I've been incredibly lucky. The good thing is that I have had two careers, and both careers I really like doing.

"On the other hand," he adds jokingly, "if I had spent more time practicing drums than playing with race cars, maybe I'd be able to write books on how to play drums properly.

"But when it comes down to it, I've never really done a day's work in my life."

"I think I've raced everything I own, well, except for that Model T, which must be the most dangerous car ever built."

The Dark Side of the…shop. Mason is just as comfortable behind the wheel or working a spanner (wrench) as he is behind a drum set. Here, he takes a break next to his best friend of thirty-five years, his Ferrari 250 GTO.

No serious Ferrari collection would be complete without a model display of every 250 GTO built!

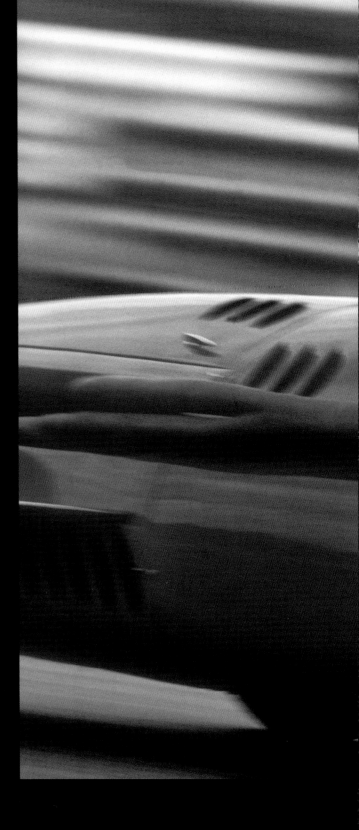

Mason substitutes his drum sticks for a steering wheel and a shift knob as often as he can manage. He races frequently in top vintage racing events in cars like this Maserati 250F Grand Prix car.

10

RACHEL
BOLAN

Skid Row's busy touring schedule has taken a toll on Bolan's driving ambitions. He'll throw this kart in the back of his Dodge pickup and race at a clay oval near his Atlanta home whenever the opportunity presents itself. Rachel Bolan collection

OPPOSITE: *Black is beautiful! Skid Row's Rachel Bolan loves the color black. He bought this ZR-1 Corvette new in 1991 when his band started making money. With only 61,000 miles, he seldom drives it these days but can't bring himself to sell it. "It's good for burning up the back roads," he says.*

SKID ROW
THAT RECKLESS-ABANDON MENTALITY

Rachel Bolan likes the color black. His hair is black, his T-shirt is black, his pants and shoes are black. Even his Corvette and pickup truck are black.

If good guys wear white hats, Bolan is a bad guy.

Plus, with a first name like Rachel, you'd have to be a badass just to survive junior high school.

Except he's not.

The founder, songwriter, and bass player for the band Skid Row is actually a low-key, cool dude.

And he is hooked on those same two passions you've read about over and over in this book: music and cars.

"I found my passion for cars and music at the same time," he says. "Or I should say they found me. Growing up in New Jersey, racing wasn't as popular as it was in the South. But as a kid I'd go to Wall Stadium with my older brother, Ritchie to watch Ray Evernham race modifieds. But the music bug hit me, too, so I went into that direction, and cars turned into my hobby."

These days, Skid Row performs about 100 concerts a year, not nearly as many as when they were at the height of their popularity in the '90s. By 1996, the group had already sold more than 20 million albums and had multiple platinum discs. The band was even invited to perform in Moscow, Russia, at the Peace Festival Concert.

But even when he and his band were living on the road, they never missed an opportunity to race.

Bolan got hooked on racing when he drove this Legends car. The car was prepared in Concord, North Carolina, by Kurt Andrews of Andrews Motorsports. Bolan no longer owns the little racer, but as he says, "I'll still jump in one occasionally when I'm up near Charlotte." Rachel Bolan collection

"We'd hit every indoor go-kart track we could find," says Bolan. "We didn't go for those kiddie karts, but the serious racing karts. There was a place just outside of Minneapolis that had the fastest indoor go-karts I'd ever driven."

Bolan's love of fast machines wasn't born in the womb, but it began not too long after. His brother Ritchie, ten years his senior, was a certified motorhead.

"He was totally my hero," he says. "He turned me onto cars at a really young age. When I was young, he and his friends would take a car apart and put it together again the same weekend. They would drag race on back roads near our house.

"Ritchie would take me to Englishtown with his friends to watch the drag races, and he turned me on to NASCAR."

Today, Bolan and NASCAR Sprint Cup champion Tony Stewart are friends. He also admires sprint car ace Danny Lasoski. And Bolan spends as much time behind the wheels of racing cars as he can.

"I love racing anything," he enthuses. "I've raced Legends Cars, Thunder Roadsters, and a Pro-Challenge Truck. Lately I'm having fun racing my go-kart on a clay surface oval track."

Bolan races with Andrews Motorsports out of Concord, North Carolina—in the heart of NASCAR country—who also prep his racing machines. He has raced at tracks in Atlanta, Georgia, and in Charlotte and Hickory, North Carolina.

"I've never raced anything like vintage Can-Am like Brian [Johnson, his friend and AC/DC vocalist], but one day I would like to."

Bolan tells with regret a story of being invited to co-drive an endurance race with Johnson at a Road Atlanta race, but he was touring and couldn't get away.

"I can see myself doing more racing events, like vintage road racing, once I have more time," says Bolan.

He has the driving credentials. Once, when invited to compete in a celebrity race in Denver, a Skip Barber Racing School certificate was required.

"I took the class at Lime Rock Park in Connecticut, and I learned so much. I learned that I had to get up for class every day at 6 a.m., and I remember a little saying they taught us: 'When in a spin, both feet in.' That class back in 1990 changed my mind about driving on the road ever since."

ONE FOR THE ROAD

When Skid Row was topping the charts, Bolan rewarded himself with a four-wheel trophy, a brand-new 1991 Corvette ZR-1. Today, twenty years later, he still has the car.

"I ordered it just before we left on tour in South America," he says. "When we got home, the car was in my garage. I think I paid $55,500 for it."

Guess what? It's black.

He's thought about selling the 61,000-mile car, but then he would take it for a drive and change his mind.

"I had always dreamed about buying a new black-on-black Corvette. This car is the only automotive reward I've ever given myself. I've had a lot of ex-girlfriends who are gone, but I'm glad this 'Vette is still with me."

Unlike his older brother Ritchie, who is a Mopar guy, Bolan prefers Chevy. When he's on the road, he'll see old cars in people's backyards in the Midwest and promise to come back and tow the car home. "I'd like to find a 1956 Chevy that I could tub out, lower, and put a huge motor inside," he dreams.

But his ultimate ride would be a 1968 Camaro RS/SS.

"It would be gloss black [big surprise . . .] with flat black rally stripes, and I'd have the biggest engine I could fit under the hood.

"I'm not worried about it being original. I'd just like something that was fast, loud, and reliable."

Bolan is hooked on racing and would like to make it his second career.

"I would love to race six months a year and tour with the band the other six months," he says. "I'd race semi-professional, but getting sponsors was tough when the economy was good; now it's really hard.

"There are so many similarities between going out to race and stepping on stage. In racing, you're sitting there in the staging lanes, waiting to go out onto the track, which is kind of like waiting in the hallway waiting to go on stage. Then all the excitement of performing is like the green flag being dropped.

"Fortunately, when I'm on stage, I don't have the fear of flipping, which is a good thing.

"I think it's the same reckless-abandon mentality."

Even though Bolan had raced Legends Cars for many years, he never got used to the horsepower. "The wheelbase was too short. Now, these Thunder Roadsters have a longer wheelbase and handle more like a real race car," he says. He raced this car on Concord Speedway's half-mile oval. Rachel Bolan collection

FUEL

ROCK AND ROLL: THE INTERSECTION OF ART AND CRAFT. ONE OF THESE ROCKERS CREATES

AUTOMOTIVE ART, AND THE OTHERS CREATE THE INSTRUMENTS THAT MAKE THE MUSIC POSSIBLE.

BUT THEY ALL SHARE ONE THING IN COMMON: A PASSION FOR ALL THINGS AUTOMOTIVE.

INJECTED

What is it about cars and guitars? Apparently an infatuation with cool cars is not the exclusive domain of musical performers. In the course of writing this book, we met a number of guitar builders—luthiers—who share the same "gearhead" gene with many of the musicians who play their instruments.

These are the guys who cut, carve, sand, and finish the wood that becomes the instruments we hear on CDs, radios, and at concerts. And they love cars almost as much as they love instruments.

WAYNE
HENDERSON

Guitars and T-Birds abound in Henderson's shop and home. His living room features samples of his two loves. The beautiful inlaid mother-of-pearl design work on this guitar neck is further reason Henderson's guitars are so sought after.

OPPOSITE: Henderson Guitars are world-renowned, and guitar players from around the world beat a path to his shop in rural Rugby, Virginia. Visitors are frequently treated to a ride in the T-Bird.

CLAPTON CAN WAIT

Located in rural Rugby, Virginia— population seven—Wayne Henderson slowly turns out some of the finest acoustic guitars in the world. As opposed to large guitar-making operations where staffs of workers each contribute one specialty to the finished instrument, Henderson builds each guitar from scratch by himself in a small brick shop next to his house.

Don't be fooled by the humble environment, however. Henderson's guitars are nothing less than world class. Some of the biggest names in rock and bluegrass music beat a path to Henderson's door and "ask" if he'll make them an instrument.

Wayne Henderson was the subject of a terrific book called *Clapton's Guitar*, by Allen St. John, which chronicled rocker Eric Clapton's ten-year journey to acquiring a Henderson guitar. The book described Henderson's careful selection of wood for the body up to and including the finished and tuned guitar being delivered to "Slowhand."

In addition to building such desirable guitars, Henderson is also a blue grass virtuoso who has performed at Carnegie Hall, all across America, Europe, and the Middle East, and even on *The Prairie Home Companion* radio show. Music and guitars are Henderson's primary passions in life.

Passion number two? His 1957 Thunderbird.

"One of my favorite things has always been a 1957 Thunderbird," Henderson explains. "I always wanted one but couldn't afford a nice one. But a good friend

ABOVE LEFT: Henderson only crafts a few guitars each year, so the waiting list can be years long. The excellent book Clapton's Guitar *documents the construction of rocker Eric Clapton's Henderson Guitar, for which he waited ten years. ABOVE RIGHT: Henderson always has finger picks in his pocket. He's primarily a guitar builder, but here he samples a rare Henderson mandolin. Each of his instruments has a unique serial number stamped inside, and his guitars sell for tens of thousands of dollars on the collector market.*

of mine, Mr. Ralph Maxwell, who is ninety years old, told me that one his friends had one sitting in a barn."

Thus began Henderson's barn-find Thunderbird adventure. The car had been sitting in a Hollywood, Florida, barn for twenty-five years. The gentleman who bought it had died, but Henderson was able to negotiate with the son.

"It was in pretty rough shape, and it was painted in a blue that T-birds didn't even come in," he recalls. "So I got it and brought it home and it sat in the garage while I negotiated some deals with people who could restore it."

Henderson didn't have the cash to have his car restored, but he had something more valuable to trade: Henderson Guitars, instruments so beloved that they are more likely to be passed on through generations than sold.

"I have one guitar in the Thunderbird's paint job, one guitar in the engine rebuild, another in the bumper replating, and one in the interior," says Henderson. "Oh, and I just had a fellow rebuild the transmission, so that makes five guitars in that car. But not too much money, except for my purchase price."

Henderson's shop is a destination for guitar collectors and bluegrass pickers. Some come to play music, but most come to hang around the shop and tell stories.

"I have lots of company," he says. "Last Sunday, a bunch of French people were here with their wives, so I took the top off the T-Bird and gave them all rides around the roads around here. I must have put on thirty miles driving them around. It's my biggest thrill, to give people rides in my car, and then pick a couple of songs for them."

Henderson is not a car collector, but the luthier has always loved the first-generation Thunderbirds. One day, he mentioned that to a friend, who said, "I know where one is."
He purchased the car and had it restored by local craftsmen, trading a total of five guitars to cover the cost of the work.

CARS AND GUITARS

JOL DANTZIG

Dantzig sold his vintage-racing B23 FIA Group 6 Chevron recently. "Racing that car was such a great experience for me," he says of the two-liter, Cosworth-powered sports racer. He's now shopping for a vintage Formula 5000 car.

OPPOSITE: By blending abstract art into the design of his guitars, Dantzig hopes to become the Chip Foose of guitars. He sells instruments to many top performers and bands like Mark Knopfler and Judas Priest and even two artists featured in this book: Brad Whitford of Aerosmith and Billy F Gibbons of ZZ Top.

JOL DANTZIG'S HOT ROD GUITARS

Think of Jol Dantzig as the Chip Foose of guitar design.

Like Foose's automotive creations, Dantzig's one-of-a-kind electric guitars are works of art that are played by the biggest names in rock and roll. He draws his inspiration for guitar design from custom car culture.

"I want to build guitars that are considered as special as Cadzilla," he explains, referring to the radical, customized Cadillac owned by ZZ Top guitarist and lead singer Billy F Gibbons. "It's all a blend of designs. Custom cars and custom guitars are a blending of design disciplines."

Dantzig's father was both a musician and a car enthusiast. "He played keyboards and the sax, but he was always tinkering in the garage. He once supercharged his Volvo 1800."

In Dantzig's case, the apple didn't fall far from the tree.

Growing up in Chicago in the 1960s, Dantzig accompanied his father to races like the US Grand Prix at Watkins Glen, New York; Illinois' Blackhawk Farms; and Meadowdale. At the same time, the teenaged Jol was buying, repairing, and selling vintage electric guitars as well as selling his own custom-designed slot-car chassis to neighborhood kids. Clearly he was an entrepreneur in the making.

Eventually he began building and selling his own guitar designs. His first was a Flying V bass, a breakthrough design for bass guitarists in 1973. He then went to work in the guitar industry before founding the Hamer brand [When?]. He sold Hamer

in 19XX and now creates custom guitars through his brand, Jol Dantzig Guitar Design.

Some four decades after he began fiddling around with vintage guitars, his own designs are now played by some of the top musicians in the industry. All four Beatles owned Dantzig-designed guitars (Ringo has two.). Aerosmith's Brad Whitford plays one, as does Billy F Gibbons, Mark Knopfler, and Joe Perry, to name but a few.

"I like to say my guitars are played by everyone from A to Z—from Air Supply to ZZ Top."

Like many guitar builders, Dantzig is an accomplished musician, inspired since his youth by Chicago bluesmen like Buddy Guy, Howling Wolf, and Muddy Waters. When he was younger, he played in clubs on weekends, but more recently, he has played on soundtracks for TV and movies. He has also performed live with Wilson Pickett.

As time from his business allowed, Dantzig began pursuing his other love: racing. He started club racing Porsches, then he moved on to vintage sports racers.

"Initially I was a European car guy," he says. "I couldn't tell the difference between a 1932 Ford and a 1939 Ford. I was only interested in the newest cars and had no interest in older models."

Then an interesting thing happened one weekend while he was racing at California's Sear's Point Raceway. "I was looking at an old Maserati with wire wheels and thought it might be real cool to get a vintage race car. I thought I could probably get an old Porsche 550 Spyder for like $5,000. Then I saw they were selling for $200,000 at the time.

"I finally got it. These cars were like an old Les Paul guitar. If I had any brains, I would have realized the value and beauty of these old cars back when I was buying old guitars, back when they were affordable."

These days, Dantzig lives in Connecticut, not far from the Lime Rock Park racetrack, where he competes from time to time. In his garage is a 1973 Porsche RS lightweight racer and a 1973 Porsche RS touring car. He also has a Norton Commando and a Ducati 750 Super Sport.

K-THX 1138

"I want to build guitars that are considered as special as Cadzilla. Custom cars and custom guitars are a blending of design disciplines."

He recently sold a B23 Chevron FIA Group 6 racer and is itching for some sort of open-wheel car. "Even though it will probably get me divorced, I'd love to race an old Formula 5000 car," he says. "But if I chicken out because of all that horsepower, I'd be happy with a Formula 3 car."

And the guy who couldn't tell the difference between a 1932 and 1939 Ford? He has become a huge hot rod enthusiast. "I feel like I'm twelve years old again, back when I was learning about guitars," says Dantzig. "Except now I'm learning about hot rods and old pickup trucks."

One new hot rod trend he really digs is the "outlaw" Porsche movement. He belongs to the R Gruppe, a

group of guys who are chopping, channeling, and souping up 356 and 911 Porsches.

"These guys will take an old 356 and install a 911 engine with two cylinders cut off, so now it's a four cylinder," he says. "They'll install 911 suspension, four-wheel disc brakes, a 915 gearbox, and forged aluminum wheels with huge offsets. The only rule for these Porsches is that there are no rules."

Dantzig creates one-off guitars in a shop that is part guitar factory, part race prep shop, and part design studio. It's a garage that most of us would be content never leaving.

Do you prefer vanilla or lime? Dantzig's garage has two Porsche 911 RS models. The green car is a proper lightweight with fiberglass bucket seats, no sound proofing, and no carpet. The white one, though, is even more hardcore and ready to race: roll bar, no rear seats, radio delete, thin metal, and thin glass.

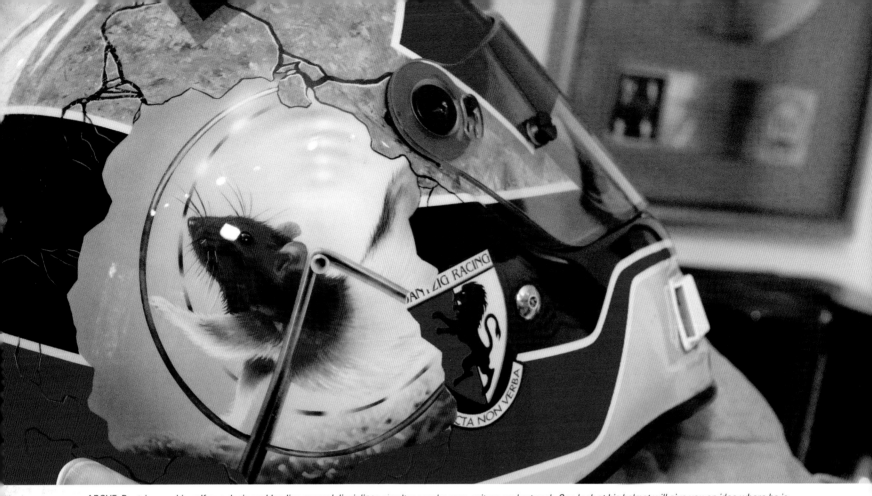

ABOVE: Dantzig sees himself as a designer blending several disciplines simultaneously: cars, guitars, and artwork. One look at his helmet will give you an idea where he is coming from: a rat spinning around in a wheel inside his skull. BELOW: Dantzig's varied interests are on display in his workshop. He works on cars and guitars in the same area, again blending his interests. "It's a blurring of disciplines," he says. OPPOSITE: Another of Dantzig's multi-disciplinary workbenches. Guitar parts and amplifier tubes on the bench, inspiration on the wall.

CARS AND GUITARS

CHRIS MARTIN

This is a replica of the original guitar factory started by Chris Martin's grandfather in Nazareth, Pennsylvania, in 1833. The vintage-looking building is connected to a museum and a modern factory, but guitars are still handmade, one at a time.

OPPOSITE: Chairman Martin is a sixth-generation guitar manufacturer and a second-generation car enthusiast. He has owned several Porsche 911s over the years, but this is his first with Porsche's PDK gearbox, which he loves.

BORN WITH CAR AND GUITAR GENES

Chris Martin can't help it; he was born with both car and guitar genes.

Martin is the sixth-generation Martin to run the family business, Martin Guitars of Nazareth, Pennsylvania. C. F. Martin Sr. left his native Germany in 1833 and began crafting guitars in New York City. Today, Martin is the largest guitar manufacturer in the world.

Chris Martin was also born into a car family. His father, Frank, and his mother, Joan, were both sports car buffs and actually met at a hill climb event in Springtown, Pennsylvania, in the early 1950s. Martin still has trophies that his mother won in the Morgan she raced.

"I think the combination of my parents' car-buff genes definitely rubbed off on me," says the fifty-six year old.

He also has terrific negotiating skills. When a traffic court judge didn't throw the book at him for speeding and passing in a restricted traffic zone, he proposed to her. Soon after, they married. All bets are off whether they would have gotten married if she had found him guilty!

Martin literally grew up in the guitar business. As a high school student, he worked in the factory during summer break. In college, he worked in a Los Angeles music store.

Under Martin's leadership, sales have increased to 95,000 guitars annually, up considerably from a low of 3,000 units in the late 1970s. Today, Martin acoustic guitars run the gamut from instruments a novice might own to rare, beautiful guitars like this ornate Model D-100 Deluxe.

When a traffic court judge didn't throw the book at Martin for speeding and passing in a restricted traffic zone, he proposed to her. Soon after, they married.

OPPOSITE: Martin's first 911. After a slew of sports cars— a Porsche 944 and Boxster, a Mazda Miata, and even a Lancia—he bought this 1990 911 Targa. Today, it is owned by a Martin employee.

"I tried to start at the bottom," he says. "What I learned is I have a great deal of respect for the people who do this all the time. And I learned I'm pretty useless with a chisel."

He went to college and graduated from Boston University with a business degree and took over the reins of the family business at age thirty.

"I was scared to death," he recalls. "Business wasn't good. During the rock-and-roll era of the 1960s and '70s, we sold 22,000 guitars a year. In the 1980s, disco knocked our business down to 3,000 guitars a year because they used a digital keyboard."

Today, Martin manufactures 95,000 guitars a year, and Chris Martin is chairman.

Over the years, his automotive passions reflected the condition of his business.

When Martin was a kid, his father owned a number of cool rides: a Shelby GT-350 convertible, a Dino Ferrari, a Lancia, and a Porsche 924. "He eventually got a 911, and even a Saab Sonnet," he said. "He bought cars without rhyme or reason; he'd just own it for a year and move on."

Early on, the younger Martin owned a Lancia and a Miata, but he promised himself that one day, when business improved, he would own a Porsche.

Martin's first Porsche, a 944 S, led to a 911, then a new Boxster, followed by a Boxster S.

"But when I had the Boxsters, I was missing the 911. For some reason, I always wanted a four-wheel-drive Porsche, because then I wouldn't need another car in the winter."

He also needed the backseat of the 911 because he drives his daughter Clare to school each morning.

Martin is clearly a Porsche man, having driven his not only to work every day, but also to track events at nearby Pocono Raceway. He has participated in a number of Bertil Roos Racing Schools, though he has yet to master the heel-and-toe technique. Which is why when Porsche announced its clutchless shifting PDK transmission, he was first in line to buy one.

"I don't miss the clutch at all," he says of his sapphire blue Carrera 4.

In his home garage, Martin keeps a small collection of interesting cars: several Porsches, a 360 Ferrari, an M3 BMW, a supercharged Land Rover, a Mercedes SLK, and a Shelby Dodge Shadow. But what he'd like to see is the PDK transmission in a GT3.

"But the car I'm really interested in isn't available in the States. That would be the hot rod Audi RS6 wagon. I have a daughter, a big dog, and I drive in the snow. I need a wagon."

A fast wagon...

12

GEORGE
FRAYNE

"In 1938 to 1939, everybody was influenced by the French style, that Talbot-Lago, Delahaye, sweeping-fenders look. How did they know that? It's straight out of Norman Bel Geddes and Raymond Loewy. They were all into streamlining. All those designs really just got me."

OPPOSITE: "Car people and cars. I've always loved them. It started when I was in a fraternity in college in 1964. We did 'Louie, Louie' at frat dances. We also did '409' and 'Little Deuce Coupe'; anything that had a harmony to it and was about cars, we did it. And it was boom! We were right there with it. And it's still like that today."

COMMANDER CODY AND
HIS LOST PLANET AIRMEN
CRASH COURSE

Whether he's talking about cars, rock music, or art, George Frayne speaks quickly, in a deep, gravelly voice you can only get after performances in hundreds of smoky bars. A skilled musician, he's also a very talented painter. "In my house," he says, "art was what was happening."

Frayne began painting portraits about fifteen years ago, using "the kind of stuff you find on the beach" for frames. After starting with oil, he switched to acrylics. "Oils never dry," he insists. "You could go up to a Rembrandt [not that he would!], pierce the surface of a red with a razor blade, and you'll find it's still wet underneath. Especially red. That's my favorite color. I'm a little fast. I'm a New Yorker.

"My dad, who's a designer, got me into the 1930s, the Bauhaus School, like Raymond Loewy and Norman Bel Geddes, leading up to Harley Earl . . . all those cats. I wasn't hip to the Italian designers until way later.

"My first car, in 1962, was a hot rod. I'd already wrecked both my parents' cars, a '53 MG and an Austin-Healey 3000. I didn't really destroy them, not like the flaming wrecks I left on the freeways in later years, but I knocked out the headlights and smashed the grille on the Healey.

"So my mom started buying Hillmans. I *really* totaled her first Hillman. No accident I've been in has ever been caused by me driving under the influence. The huge, spectacular accidents I had were in performance cars. They all happened when I was sober, and [it was] usually in the morning. It started with my going off to college.

"I bought a Ballantine Ale beer tap, screwed it right onto the shift lever, and drove off to the University of Michigan in my turquoise-and-white '55 Chevy Bel Air. It blew up, right in the U of M gas station. We thought the whole gas station would go. That was the reason there are no more gas stations in the middle of campus any more. I still don't know how the fire in the car started. It had *nothing* to do with me smoking cigarettes in the gas station. Absolutely nothing.

"I always liked fast cars. I even took a car out to Islip Speedway. One time I did 0–60 in 7.2 seconds in a '62 Austin-Healey. I was proud of myself. Now a baby carriage can do that in 3.5 seconds. But I was happy with it. Later I did 125 miles per hour in the Austin-Healey with four crazed lunatics in it. It was as fast as I could possibly want to go in that car.

"I had three 1955 Ford station wagons." (Old pictures show one in camo paint with Flying Tiger shark's teeth.) "One blew up on the Jones Beach thruway, so I put the plates on another one, which blew up on the Pennsylvania Turnpike. The third one blew up too. It was part of being a college kid. It took years before I figured out what the actual function of the dipstick was. I've gone through forty cars. My friend John sold me a '58 Volvo. It ran for two weeks. Someone gave me a '38 Packard. It ran for two days. Someone else gave me a '53 Ford pickup. He said, 'If you can start it, it's yours.' It started right up.

"Living in Berkeley, California, I had a '49 Indian Chief, and I was working on my umpteenth car, a '63 Cadillac with no brakes. I was out in Marin, going down a hill, and I crashed it right into a house owned by Gary 'Chicken' Hirsh, the drummer for [Country Joe and] the Fish. I took the plates off and ran for my life. It was belching smoke. I was a hippie, and driving a '63 Cadillac back then was like 'selling out' to the Maaaaan. I thought, 'I *have* to get a cool car.'

"That happened after I had just gotten my first paycheck for 'Hot Rod Lincoln,' when I saw a four-door Jaguar 3.8S painted chrome yellow. For Berkeley, it was perfect. My first real car, it had knockoffs and it was wonderful. But I neglected to put oil into it. You had to actually change the oil! Dumping quarts in continually doesn't really work. The red light went on.

"One of my first car paintings was called Last Date. *It was a front grille view of an Edsel and a train. That's all. Someone saw it, and I did a commission, and then I did a guy's AC Cobra. Then I started doing my first large paintings."*

You'd think a guy with a master's degree would know better, but no . . . That car blew two rods in the middle of the Richmond Bridge. We rebuilt the engine, but the transmission died. It was a '67 Jaguar; they blew a lot of transmissions. Mine was dead as a doughnut, right in downtown San Rafael.

"There was an Alfa Romeo dealer right there. He's not there anymore. He left in 1983. A 1979 GTV was $7,900 new, and I had $8,000 in my checking account, so I just went in there and drove off with it. I loved that car, but I didn't have the best luck with Alfas."

Painting and cars were a natural progression for Frayne. "My dad painted Duesenbergs and other old cars in watercolors. I'd seen them when I was a kid, and I always loved them. The Duesy had a straight 8, like my '51 Pontiac that I traded for a '51 Cadillac.

That car blew up on the way home from New York. And I had two joints in my pocket. When the car blew up, a cop found the joints. He took me right to the State Penitentiary. I was in solitary confinement for three days. It was the first narcotics bust in Carlisle, Pennsylvania. They couldn't believe it. A drug addict was coming through their county with tons of marijuana!

"In the sixties, welding bumpers together as abstract sculpture was very popular. I went to a place called Economy Binder in Ann Arbor. They'd cut up parts and dump them in the back. I'd pull up in my pickup, cruise over to the auto lot, and get a couple of tailfins and tail [rear end] cones. I'd cut them in half, weld them back together, and they'd look like a Henry Moore abstract, but in steel."

"Acrylic in the summer? Forget it. It dries as you're putting it on the brush. You can leave the brush stuck to the canvas if you want to."

"I was in Marin County for twenty years before it got too expensive, just like Aspen; everyone from out of town moved in. There was a diminishing number of rebels. It was getting testy. And I wasn't from there anyway. People who were born and raised in Stinson Beach couldn't afford to live there anymore. Besides, I blew the big real estate deal. There was a house with a pool on the side of a cliff for $75,000. My lawyer said, 'I can get it for you for $70K.' It didn't happen. But the same lawyer got me $125 grand for using my face on ZigZag cigarette rolling papers. If they'd come to me, it wouldn't have cost that much.

"I've been driving minivans for the last twenty years, and I haven't hurt myself one bit. And I haven't gotten any speeding tickets. My New York driver's license (I had to switch over when I came back in 1998) has no points!

"I still do between eighty-five to 100 gigs a year. People want to hear the old stuff. The Rolling Stones did a show; I had to pay a hundred bucks to see it. They came out and did forty-five minutes from their new CD and left. Everybody was pissed. They don't want to hear your new shit. They want to hear the stuff they already know. In a small club, you can say, let's try something new, but for a big show, fuck no. They want to hear 'Hot Rod Lincoln.' I can say, 'You've never heard this song before, but it's about trucks.' And I'll get away with it.

"NASCAR did a poll of writers as to what their favorite car songs would be. And 'Hot Rod Lincoln' was everybody's favorite automobile song. I still get a lot of publicity from it."

CRASHING THREE ALFAS

"My first Alfa GTV was perfect. If you live in San Francisco, you've got to have a performance car. There are so many great drives. I've had two wrecks in Alfas there, just going to the airport. I was late one day and misjudged a turn at six o'clock in the morning. I hit a tree, so I left the car and just called a cab.

"I came back and bought another GTV. That's the car where I had a fabulous crash. It was 9:30 in the morning in 1978. I was coming down Highway 1 and there was a pickup truck in my lane. I wasn't late; I wasn't going fast. But there was a little sand in the road and I spun. Suddenly I was going backwards, and there was nothing I could do about it. The car flipped, landed on the passenger side, which was badly dented in, then it flipped again, hit this tree and stopped. My suitcase flew out and went over the cliff. I got back up to Highway 1, stuck out my thumb, and I made the flight. My manager didn't believe me; he sent a photographer and they ran the pictures in *Rolling Stone* magazine.

"Of course, I had to get another one, my third. This one was a '79. In just three years, it was rotted out like crazy and one of the axles just fell off, whoooommmppp!!!, going over the hill. It was just lying there in a heap on the road that goes down from Mill Valley to Stinson Beach.

"After my third Alfa blew up, I was driving in Europe and I saw all those German cars. I couldn't paint on tour, so I bought a Canon camera and just took photographs."

"I always liked fast cars. I even took a car out to Islip Speedway. One time I did 0–60 in 7.2 seconds in a '62 Austin-Healey. I was proud of myself. Now a baby carriage can do that in 3.5 seconds."

Frayne's work is frequently on display at the Saratoga Automobile Museum in Saratoga Springs, New York. This painting of a Lancia Aurelia B24 Spider hangs above a Lamborghini 400GT 2+2, formerly owned by Rockin' Garages co-author Ken Gross.

COLLECTORS

IF ONE IS GOOD, TWELVE ARE BETTER. THESE LUCKY ROCKERS HAVE INTRIGUING COLLECTIONS AND GREAT STORIES ABOUT HOW THEY BECAME GEARHEADS AND WHAT MOTIVATES THEIR PURSUIT OF CERTAIN CARS AND BIKES. THEIR PASSION GREW FROM THE SAME BOYHOOD DREAMS ALL ENTHUSIASTS HAVE, BUT THESE MUSICIANS ARE LIVING THE DREAM.

AND CRUISERS

13

BILLY JOEL

20th Century Cycles is one block from the classic Oyster Bay railroad station (soon to become a rail museum) and a couple of blocks from Long Island Sound. It's a display for Joel's collection, and he makes it clear that he doesn't sell motorcycles.

OPPOSITE: Billy Joel outside his 20th Century Cycles. He's standing with an Indian-built Royal Enfield that's had the full-on 1960s café treatment. Behind Joel are a 1952 Fiat Topolino (left) and a 1941 Chevy flatbed truck, which he uses to haul bikes.

YOU MAY BE RIGHT, I MAY BE CRAZY

Billy Joel blames it all on a neighborhood kid named Mark. Mark left his beloved Triumph 650cc Bonneville in Joel's care when he was shipped off to fight in Vietnam. It was 1967, the Summer of Love, and to this day, Joel can't get that bike out of his head.

"It was black and silver," recalls the six-time Grammy winner. "I kept the bike clean, covered, and running. But it pissed oil all over the concrete floor. And the Lucas 'Prince of Darkness' electrics were terrible."

Despite those foibles, today, forty-five years later, Joel has built a collection of bikes that, at least in spirit, resemble that very Triumph.

Joel grew up in blue-collar Levittown, on Long Island, in a house on a quarter-acre lot his father bought on the GI Bill for $40 down. The twelve-year-old wanted a motorbike in the worst way. Even a Briggs & Stratton engine on a Schwinn bicycle frame would have been fine. "But I didn't have a garage, tools, or knowledge of how to build one," he says. Looking out the window, he'd watch the "rich kids" ride their Whizzer motorbikes down the street while he sat inside practicing piano.

The motorcycle industry's loss was undoubtedly the music industry's gain.

Some years later, Joel saw a Norman Rockwell painting on the cover of a *Saturday Evening Post* showing three little boys marveling at a full-dress Harley. "It had fringed mudflaps, a turkey tail, and a gigantic buddy seat," says Joel. "And I realized I could have been any one of those kids."

Joel finally got his motorcycle when his neighbor Mark returned from Vietnam and sold him the Bonneville cheap. He never bothered to register or insure the Triumph; he just rode it with Mark's old license plate. Joel's focus had moved on to music.

Joel's eclectic 20th Century Cycles collection reflects his varied two-wheeled interests. The collection includes a Vincent Rapide, a Whizzer motorbike, and dozens of Yamahas, Kawasakis, and Royal Enfields.

From the time he was fifteen, he had been in rock-and-roll bands. The Echos, the Lost Souls, the Hassles, and even a heavy-metal band called Attila. "Go ahead and Google 'the worst rock and roll album ever' and Attila will be mentioned," he says. "We performed classics like 'Godzilla,' 'Amplifier Fire,' and 'Revenge is Sweet.' But my voice couldn't handle it because I was screaming like Brian Johnson from AC/DC."

The heavy-metal life of performing in New York City clubs until 4 a.m. wore Joel down, so he set his sights on a career as a songwriter. "I'd write and perform like James Taylor, Elton John, Joni Mitchell, and Harry Nilsson. So I signed a deal and moved to California."

But life got complicated on the West Coast. His contract was terrible, and he worked nonstop. "I got married, lived in Malibu, and didn't ride a motorcycle for years," he recalls. Not until he moved back to Long Island in the mid-1970s did he again scratch his motorcycle itch.

"I tried to write a motorcycle song once, but it's hard to make something rhyme with cycle. I've never been able to figure it out."

"I'd hang out at Ghost Motorcycles in Port Washington and bought a house in Oyster Bay," he says. "I had just released [The] Stranger, which was a big album, so for the first time, I had some money."

In 1977, Joel, then twenty-seven bought a Yamaha 400 Special and thought life couldn't get any better—at least until he traded up to a Yamaha 750 Virago, and then to his first Harley-Davidson, an AMF-era Sportster. "When I bought the Harley, I thought I had arrived," he says.

The Sportster gave way to a 1981 Harley FLH Electra Glide. "When I bought a new bike, I'd keep my old ones. But once in a while, I'd have an Elvis moment and just give one away," he says. "'Here, buddy, you can have my old bike. Thank you very much.'"

THE CRASH

While riding his FLH in 1982, Joel stopped at a traffic light on Route 110 in Huntington, Long Island. When Joel's light turned green, an elderly woman ran her red light just as Joel entered the intersection. He T-boned the woman's car, crushing his left thumb between the handgrip and the gas tank, before he launched over the car's roof.

"The impact pulverized the bone in my left thumb and pulled my right wrist out of its socket," he says. "I'm bleeding, my hands didn't work, and a police officer asks me for my license. So I told him to pull my wallet out of my pocket. He looks at my license, then yells to the woman 'Hey, lady, you just hit Billy Joel!'

"So I'm sitting there in shock, and bystanders start asking me for an autograph. 'Yeah, sure, let me sign it in blood.'

"I was flown by helicopter and landed in Riverside Park near Columbia Presbyterian Hospital in New York, where like 100 police officers were waiting to give me an escort to the emergency room. They must have thought the President was injured."

Joel was laid up for two months. When he recovered, the Piano Man had to learn to play the keyboard differently because the end bone in his left thumb had been removed. "It's just a pile of mush, so I had to learn to play the keyboard with the side of that thumb instead of the tip.

"But, hey, it's only rock and roll."

Soon Joel was riding again, with casts on both arms and one on his leg. Once, following a day of riding after

Something the young William Joel longed for when he was growing up in Levittown, Long Island; this vintage Whizzer motorbike is similar to what kids were riding around his neighborhood while he was stuck inside practicing piano.

THE BOSS' BIKE

"Bruce [Springsteen] is always looking for a character bike. He has one of the new Triumph Bonnevilles, which is a great bike. I told him about our shop, so he came down in the middle of the winter. It's freezing—minus-five-degrees—and he wants to take out my Sacred Cow bobber. I said, 'Are you crazy?' It's so cold, and he had no gear, just a helmet. After a ride, he came back and said, 'I want you to build me that bike.' So he gave us the specs, and we're almost finished with it. It started out as a Kawasaki W650. The frame is black and the tank will be metalflake gold. Man, he's hard core."

OPPOSITE: Sacred Cow is not a shy bike in either appearance or exhaust note. Joel's pal Bruce Springsteen tried this bike on a cold winter's day and liked it so much that he asked Joel to build one for him.

LEFT: Joel on a bike is a familiar site in downtown Oyster Bay. If the weather is agreeable, Joel rides every day, at least one hour, and if his schedule allows, as many as eight hours. He's astride Sacred Cow, his favorite "hot rod," which started life as a Kawasaki W650 then was modified by 20th Century Cycles to resemble a 1950s-era bobber like those featured in the classic biker flick The Wild Ones.

ABOVE: Joel posing for a glamour shot on a late '70s Sportster. Jim Houghton

RIGHT: The curly hair tells you this is a dated photo. Joel displays some of his early bikes on the lawn of his Oyster Bay home, including, from left, a Sportster, a Yamaha Virago, and a Shovelhead FLH. Dan Weaks

his accident, he parked his Harley in the driveway and hobbled toward his front door. He tripped in a gopher hole, jammed his foot, and fell down. And he couldn't get up.

"I'm lying on the ground ten feet from my front door and can't move. So I'm on my back for hours and the sun starts going down. I started laughing hysterically. 'They're going to find my starved skeleton right outside my front door!'"

Eventually he dislodged his leg and hobbled into his house, but his injuries likely added to his congenital hip and back problems.

"Certainly bike suspensions didn't do my back any favors—bang, bang, bang. Every time I hit a bump, I was compressing my spine."

BRANCHING OUT

After recovering from his motorcycling and gopher-hole injuries, Joel expanded his riding repertoire to include BMWs, Ducatis, and Moto Guzzis. He decided to stop riding older bikes because "when you're riding, you can't think about whether the brake or shifter is on the right or left because if you think, you're dead. It must be instinctive. I needed to ride bikes where the brake is always on the right and the shifter is always on the left. The British bikes had it all the other way around."

Joel prefers café racers and bobbers. "With café racers, you beef up the brakes and beef up the handling, and they become very high performance machines," he says.

From a distance, this "Harley" may look vintage, but the bike is actually new. Built to resemble a 1949 Panhead, this modern-retro machine features disk brakes, a 12-volt electrical system, an S&S engine, and replica softtail frame. It's typical of many of the bikes in Joel's collection; a melding of the modern with the classic.

Joel has never had a Japanese-bike phobia. "They are lighter, better, cheaper, and their engineering is brilliant," he says. "And Japanese bikes got more people into motorcycles, which we should all be happy about."

After selling a number of interesting bikes in the 1980s and 1990s—a move he deeply regrets—he decided to begin collecting an assortment of bikes that are personally special to him, regardless of their investment value.

Today he builds retro bikes that resemble that precious Triumph Bonneville he once babysat for his neighbor all those years ago. He owns 20th Century Cycles, a non-business, non-museum located off Main Street in Oyster Bay. ("I don't sell anything, so it's not a business, and I ride all my bikes, so it's not a museum…")

Joel purchased his 1978 Ducati 900 SS from Nashville-based motorcycle collector Somer Hooker. It's one of Billy's favorite bikes, and it has the look that he tries to replicate in his "café" conversions.

The "Sacred Cow" bobber is built around a Kawasaki W650 twin from the early 2000s. After a freezing winter test ride, Joel's pal Bruce Springsteen ordered one for himself.

"Oyster Bay used to be part of Long Island's Great Gatsby Gold Coast," says Joel. "My mother used to bring my sister and me here to the beach when we were kids."

Fearing that his adopted hometown was slipping economically, Joel put his bikes on public display in an effort to rejuvenate downtown businesses. 20th Century Cycles is open weekends from 10 a.m. to 4 p.m.

Joel, the designer, and his restorer, Alex Puls, convert Yamaha and Kawasaki twins into Bonneville look-alikes. Or they'll modify a late-model, India-made Royal Enfield into a vintage scrambler or trials bike. They've also converted a 1960s BMW R60 into a World War II German Army replica, adding a Russian Ural sidecar and painting it Luftwaffe Gray. "Everyone likes the way old things look, but they love the way new things work," says Joel.

Surrounded by all these great bikes, one wonders which is Joel's dream bike, the one he desires more than any other. It was like asking someone which child is their favorite.

"Moto Guzzis are my personal favorites," he says after much contemplation. "I once rented a V7 Classic in Lake Como in Italy. That would be my all-time favorite ride.

"But I once owned a 1981 Ducati Mike Hailwood replica. It was a first-year model. I was riding it home on the causeway near my house one day. I thought I was going about 70 mph, but when I looked down at the speedometer, I was going twice that fast—140 mph. It was the last time I rode that bike. But I wish I had it back."

Joel opened 20th Century Cycles near Main Street in Oyster Bay, Long Island, New York, in order to attract tourists to the small village on Long Island's former Gold Coast. The sixty-five-bike collection is open and free to the public on weekends.

Joel rides thousands of
miles a year, often renting
bikes during concert tour
stops. And he knows his
motorcycle stuff as well as
any enthusiast. He can rattle
off history, serial numbers,
and values with the best of
them. Joel scans eBay and
motorcycle websites on a
daily basis searching for
"diamonds in the rough."

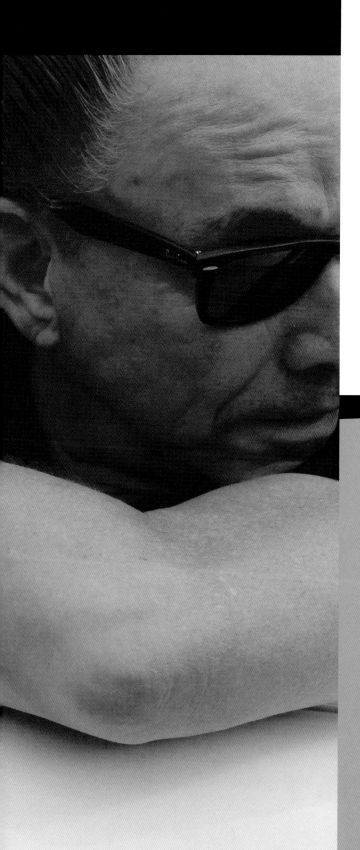

14

JIMMIE
VAUGHAN

FABULOUS THUNDERBIRDS
TEXAS COOL

With his slicked back hair, dark shades, and black jeans, Texas bluesman Jimmie Vaughan looks as though he's just stepped out of the early 1960s. He speaks authoritatively with a sloooow drawl. His well-hidden Austin garage is filled with authentic hot rods and customs. He's given a lot of thought to selecting the cars he has and carefully overseen their modifications.

"I was born in '51," Jimmie says. "I don't remember not liking cars. It's always been about cars with me. I started playing guitar 'cause I thought maybe I could get me a car. As a little kid, I used to drive around with my Uncle Joe in his '53 Ford, and he'd say, 'That's a '47 Packard; that's a '51 Ford.'

"As a kid, I built model cars, and my mother kept pictures of cars that I drew." He was fascinated with customs and the guys who drove them. "They seemed like guys who could stay up all night," he recalls.

"I ran off when I was fourteen. Instead of getting my license at fifteen like everybody else, I was a total guitar player for several years. I was in a band, playing anywhere I could. When I was twenty-one, all the car stuff came back. I got my driver's license and started up.

The essence of cool . . . custom guys knew girls didn't want to be scared to death in hot rods— they liked cruising low and slow, making the scene in a cool ride with a guy who knew the score. Jimmie nails it.

"My first car was a yellow-and-white '56 Buick Century Riviera four-door hardtop, a four-holer. It had accessory hubcaps and glass-packs. I did that stuff to it the first day.

"But my first car was supposed to be my Uncle's '53 Ford convertible. It sat beside his house, and he was gonna give it to me. But I'd run off to be a musician, and it got towed away. I got a DUI in the Buick, and I had to sell it to pay the lawyer. That makes for a good story . . . live and learn, huh?"

CUSTOM CULTURED

"The first custom car I really did is my '51 Chevy Fleetline. I've had it for thirty years. I agonized over whether to do a mild custom with that car or get a '40 Ford. I picked the Chevy because I was into customs. I'd read about George Barris. That's really all I thought about. When I started building model cars, I tried to customize all of them; they were lowered, nosed, and decked.

"My Chevy has everything but a chop. It was done two or three times until it was right. I usually do everything two or three times before I get it right. Seems like I'm getting better, but a lot of stuff I've learned the hard way.

"I was really into the '60s. Remember that lavender '56 Olds from Gene Winfield, Dennis Reinero's hardtop? *That* influenced the color. Years later, this guy walked up to my Chevy. 'That's sooooo beautiful,' he said. 'That's the color of my girlfriend's underwear in high school.' I said, 'Thank you, man.' *That's* a good compliment.

"I talked about chopping that car, but with these fastbacks, you don't really get anything [more]. I think it's beautiful. They didn't use skirts on 'em when I did this car, so the fenders have Ford-style flares. Rod Powell made the [plastic] taillights in his oven, and his wife got really pissed off at him 'cause it made a smell. I just did stuff that made sense. The back is all rounded; the two-piece hood is molded and peaked. That's all very hard to do right. There are thirty-one Corvette grille teeth. This was before you could buy 'em. I had to get 'em in junkyards and trim 'em to fit."

Look closely—Jimmie's '63 Riviera is chopped oh-so-subtly, improving the already great look of a GM classic that styling boss Bill Mitchell first offered to Cadillac, and then built for Buick.

ABOVE: A study in contrasts, Jimmie's '32 Ford 5-window coupe with its hot flathead, is a generation removed from his chopped Caddy with its Latham-blown big-block. Either way, that's how Jimmie rolls.

Every serious hot rodder needs a '40 Ford. Jimmie shows co-author Ken Gross his "Folkstone Gray" DeLuxe Business Coupe. Lowered, mostly stock with accessory trim rings, it's awaiting a serious engine swap. "Forties don't need any bodywork; they're just right," Vaughan notes.

RIGHT: Jimmie's '35 Ford three-window coupe is an understated road warrior with a healthy flathead, "Montella Brown" finish, and conservative blackwalls on "Poppy Red" Kelsey wire wheels.

BELOW: Would you drive a '32 five-window from Austin to L.A.? Jimmie made it in this coupe and reports he had a ball. "I shouted out loud, 'I'm drivin' to L.A. in a '32 Ford!'" he says. The coupe's hot flatty never missed a beat. Jimmie likes to drive his cars.

"I don't remember not liking cars. It's always been about cars with me. I started playing guitar 'cause I thought maybe I could get me a car.

Jimmie's quick to hand out credits. "I couldn't have done any of this stuff without my guys. Gary Howard saved me on this car." It's got all the era-correct custom touches: Buick side trim, a '50 Pontiac bumper. "Vernon McKean did the pearl white tuck and roll upholstery." He smiles. "It's a bitchin' job."

Jimmie's '54 Ford hardtop Victoria is arguably one of the best ever of its genre. "With this car, although I knew about all that stuff from reading the little books, I'd already been thinking about it. It looks Ford, but it's still custom. I bought it in Paso Robles as a 54,000-mile car in primer. They'd done it in a couple of weeks in a muffler shop. It was cool, just slammed, and it was a '54 Ford. That's what I wanted. But I had to do the grille over."

The grille opening uses trim elements from a '55 Ford to make it appear wider. Taillights are from a '56 Olds Rocket frenched, ever-so-slightly, in extended fenders. "With customs, the whole idea is to make 'em look better. Make 'em look cool. But it's really hard to do that, because Detroit was making some beautiful stuff.

"I really dig the early '60s. I try to create stuff from that time period, but I like to do my own cars rather than duplicate actual customs from that era. I'm a custom

guy who fell in love with Fords at the end," Jimmie confesses, pointing to his '35 Ford three-window coupe. "I drove it to L.A. and back," he says proudly.

"When I was driving down the freeway in this '35, I lost those axle retainer keys. Now it's got Ford late model axles and juice brakes, but it's still all traditional. There's no radio, no A/C, nothing. It is what it is. Besides, it's good for the musical thing. When you're driving down the highway and you don't have all that stuff, you gotta use your mind. Or you're free to dream."

He's got a cheat sheet in each car. "I get in one, and I forget how the other ones work," he admits. "You gotta remember how to start it, how to shift it." Jimmie's modest about the fact that his cars are acclaimed. He's won the Harry Bradley Award. He's been on the cover of *R&C* and featured in *The Rodder's Journal*. "I've won my class a couple times at the GNRS." He shakes his head, almost as if he still can't believe it.

One of Jimmie's big influences was Los Angeles' Larry Watson in the 1960s. His '63 Buick Riviera is slammed and painted lime gold with a little metalflake, and it's chopped several inches. "I never wanted to chop 'em to where they looked goofy," Jimmie explains. "If you chop 'em too much, then they look as though they're broken. I want people to come up to the car and wonder. Now guys'll say, 'That's not chopped.' They'll stand alongside your car at a car show and argue with you. I always wanted a Riviera. A friend of mine's dad had one when I was in high school. It turned my head. Still does.

"Here's the thing: This is an absolute fantasy. I *can't* do this. It's impossible. I wanted a car when I was a kid. I didn't think I was gonna get a car, ever. That's all I thought about. If I had a car like *that*, and la-di-da-di-dah, what would I do with it? One of my cars on the cover of a magazine? It's the same with being a blues guitar player. Dreams come true, if you work on it. *That's* what it's about.

"A lot of musicians are car enthusiasts, but I was into cars first [before being a musician]. The first thing

Fins and chrome go hand-in-hand here. The rounded contours and multiple Corvette grille teeth on Jimmie's '51 Chevy are in marked contrast to the crisp, edgy perfection of his '61 Cadillac hardtop. Both have been magazine-feature cars.

ABOVE: A '51 Fleetline interior melds a modified stock dash panel with a sleek Impala steering wheel. Customizers took the best of Detroit and subtly made it better. Jimmie's an expert on classic customizing, as evidenced by his cars. RIGHT: Gary Howard (left) built Jimmie's killer '61 Caddy, the Ford hardtop, and other Vaughan rides. The Cad was meant to look like a car GM could have built, only lower, faster, and way sharper.

RIGHT: Jimmie's owned his fastback '51 Chevy Fleetline for thirty years. Understated, beautifully finished and slammed, it looks as through it just rolled out of Rod & Custom; and with this cover story, it did.

I thought was maybe I could get really good on this guitar so I can get a car. Make some records, buy a car, and split. So 'buy a car and split' became my mantra.

"I had to play guitar first, which I love equally. What's not to like about it? But I had the hot rod magazines tucked into my books at school. They were like little handbooks. I was one of those guys."

For Jimmie, driving his cars is special. "This '32 five-window coupe is another dream," he says. "I drove it up to L.A. and back. The whole time I'm driving, I'm screaming at the top of my lungs, 'I'M DRIVING TO L.A. IN A '32 5-WINDOW! WITH A FLATHEAD! IT'S A DREAM COME TRUE.' It's got steel packs, an Isky 400JR cam in a French block. It's stroked, so it's pretty big for a flathead." He starts it up; it sounds bitchin'.

"I've always liked Fords and Chevys. I've probably got my yaya's out now on customs. You get older, and you start thinking, 'I don't have much time. I'd better do that thing I was gonna do before,' but then you get overwhelmed, being blessed to be able to do what you love."

THE COOLEST CADILLAC EVER

Jimmie's most famous custom is his 1961 Cadillac Coupe de Ville. Everything he knows and likes came together in this car. "Look at that paint job," he says, "and you think of Winfield or Watson, especially on a '60s car. In the mid-60s, they did a lot of pearl and candy paint jobs. And Junior (Conway) is famous for doing perfect candy paint. It was all that L.A. kind of thing. A slammed stance, Bellflower (external exhaust) tips, they go with these kind of cars.

"I thought, if Pininfarina had done a '61 Caddy coupe, what would it look like? The top is chopped quite a bit. But it was too tall stock. One of the rumors I heard was that LBJ wanted to wear his hat in the car, so the roof was originally high. It's probably bullshit, but it's a good story.

"This is my ultimate idea of what a '60s Caddy would be. But it's got a five-speed, and slicks . . . you don't want to go out when it's raining," he laughs. "Those big Stewart-Warner instruments? They didn't come that way. Lee Pratt made that panel. There's a 526-cid big-block from a '74 Eldorado, and the hood's been modified so it opens pancake-style, like on some Ferraris. It had a Latham axial flow blower and side-draft Webers originally, but that was too much for this simple guy.

"This car is very Italian," Jimmie adds, "I look at pictures and do research. When I did the Cad, I got all those Italian books. But you need to know where to stop. I added the flamethrowers (driving lights), but you don't fool with that grille. It's Cadillac already. You don't want to be screwing around too much with a Cadillac," he muses. His Coupe de Ville is a Cad with an attitude, but it retains the marque's spirit.

Vaughn's hammered '61 Cad hardtop has so many modifications we'd need the whole book to detail them. A Latham-blown Caddy big-block, a snake-belly stance, massive piecrust slicks, and Bellflower tips tell you all you need to know.

Postcard picture perfect. Vaughan's slammed and sleek '54 Ford hardtop was subtly modified by Gary Howard, with extended front and rear fenders, Olds Rocket taillights, cool flared skirts, a creamy white finish, and a silver roof.

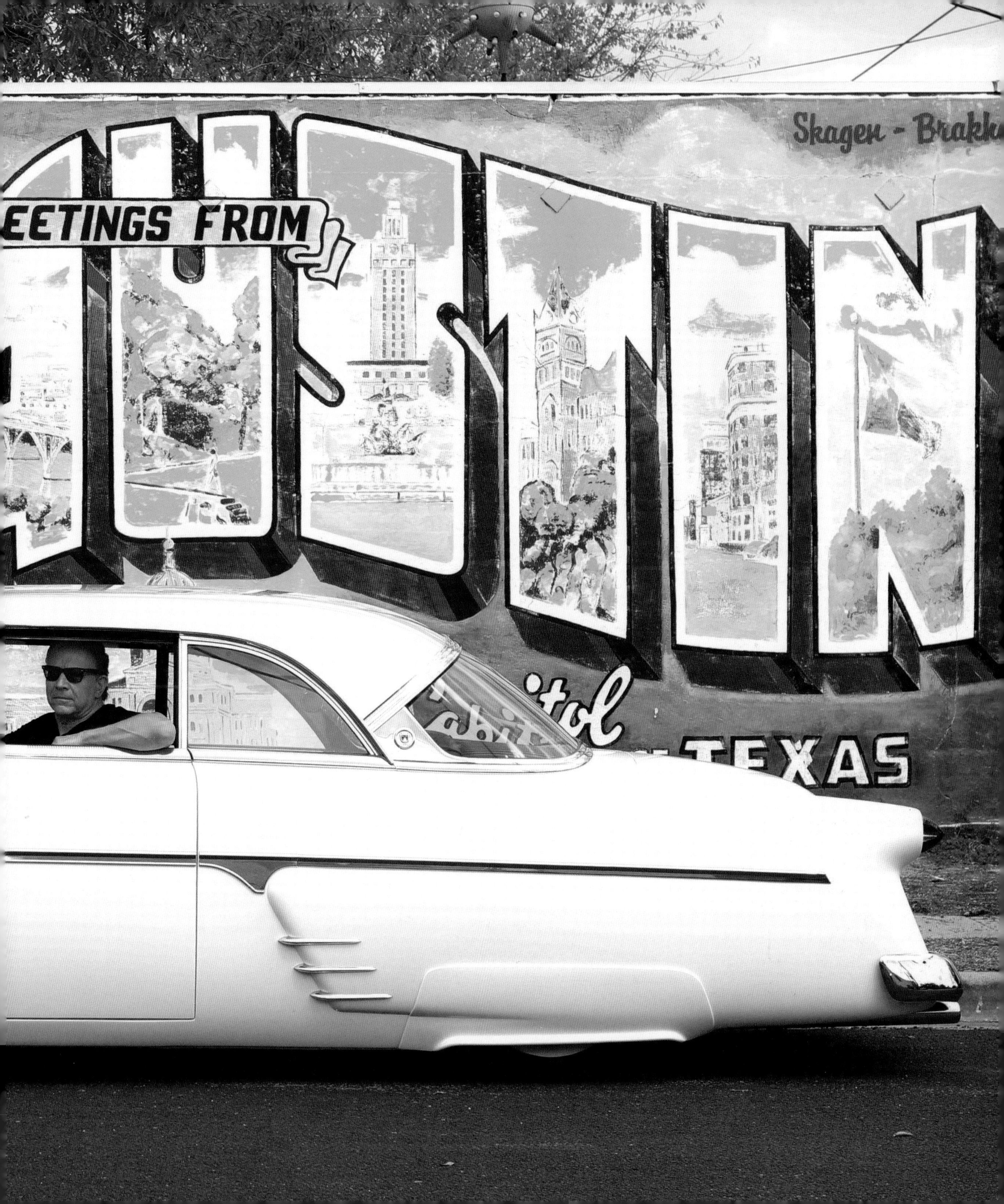
EETINGS FROM
Skagen - Brakk
TEXAS

15

MICK FLEETWOOD

The Austin 7's tiny 750 cc four-cylinder is rated at seven taxable horsepower, hence its name. "I know it's not worth lots of money," Mick says, "but what it means to me is what it's all about."

OPPOSITE: A tall man with a tiny car, Mick found his Austin on the streets of London, and left the owner a note saying he wanted to buy it. A few years later, he received the fateful call saying that it was for sale. Millions of Austin 7s were sold in Britain and licensed for production in many countries, including Japan. Fleetwood has owned Jags, Bristols, Ferraris, Porsches, and many other fine cars, but he loves his Austin 7 just as much. Maybe more.

FLEETWOOD MAC
REMEMBRANCE OF THINGS PAST

AS TOLD TO KEN GROSS

My automotive interest grew out of a quiet appreciation of cars my father had. He was a Royal Air Force pilot. We didn't have any money, but he always managed to have a lovely old MG. When I first went to London, at age sixteen, I was around a lot of art students, artists, and musicians in Nottinghill Gate. I think I probably got the bug then, well and truly.

My first car was a second-hand London taxi, a great vehicle to put my drum kit in. And I drove a beautiful old XK120 roadster for years. Even when I was totally broke, I managed to keep it going. Had I known it would now be worth a lot of money, I'd have tried to keep it. I've always dreamed of having lovely motorcars, especially ones that are not very well known. I used to have Bristol 401s, and I had a car that's no longer made called an Alvis. The Duke of Edinburgh still has one. They were never very much money, but they were beautifully made. The one old car I still have is my 1930 Austin 7.

A bass player friend was in a blues band called Savoy Seven. On the way to see him, I would pass this little Royal Blue Austin on a London street. One day I left a note saying I'd fallen in love with the car and said, if ever your car needs a home, phone this number. Two years later, my mother called. "I got this weird phone call from this guy saying that you left a very heartfelt note on his car."

'Course when I left the note, I had no money, but by then Fleetwood Mac had started and I was doing quite well. So I phoned, and lo and behold it was the guy.

He said, "I always remembered this note, and I'm moving and I can't find a place for the car. Do you still want to buy it?" Of course, I did.

The Austin 7 is a tiny, tiny car—an everyman's car. It literally has only a 7-hp engine, but it's built like a tank. It stayed with me all through my early days in London. For a whole year, I couldn't afford to put a new starter motor in it, so I used to push it, run, jump in, and shove it in gear.

When I went to America in the '70s, I left it at Eric Clapton's—Eric is my ex–brother in law—and said, "I'm disappearing and need somewhere to put my old car." He said, "I'll put it in my stable, and you pick it up whenever." About sixteen years later, I got a call from Eric's manager Roger Forrester, ''cause I was in the throes of wild rock-and-roll stardom, and truthfully I'd forgotten that I even had it. The Austin had been out in the open air in his orchard for ten years. I anticipated that it was completely done for and useless.

But I went down to see it, 'cause I wanted to sort of bury it, because it used to be such a big part of my life. Amazingly, it had bird's nests in it. The engine

had seized up, and the tires were flat. But there was no rust. I found a mechanic who restored Bugattis and racecars. I asked if he would come look at my little lady and see if it was worth saving. They took it all apart, and luckily the chassis and the fundamental things on the car were not rotten at all.

My most poignant car story, the fact that she's safe and in the garage, is that Austin. It's a huge signpost in my whole adult life. I know it's not worth lots of money, but what it means to *me* is what we're talking about. It's in concours condition now. I use it at least twice a week in Hawaii. My ninety-five-year-old mother loves it. I put a nice riding hat on her, we go out for breakfast, and we take the old Austin. It's very much a part of the family.

I've always had older cars; I redid old MGs, then I got into Porsches. On one of the tours, I bought a 1965 Ferrari 275 GTB. I drove the Ferrari in England, then shipped it to the States and had it for years. When the car boom happened, I sold it to some Japanese chap for a lot of money. I really, really regret that. Of course, it's worth way more now. It's one of the most

MICK FLEETWOOD ON THE MERCEDES-BENZ 300SL GULLWING

I really love the new SLS Gullwing Mercedes. It reminds me of another moment in time when my father was in the Royal Air Force and we were posted in Norway. My sister and I and my father went to Stuttgart on the train. Dad had ordered a not very exotic but very practical 180 diesel, brand new from the factory. I remember going to the factory and seeing, of course, the unbelievable museum there and seeing cars on their racetrack. I was very young, but I absolutely remember my father picking up the car. We went around the Mercedes factory, and then we drove back to Oslo: me, my sister, and my dad. It was our special treat with our father. That car eventually made it back to England, and Dad used it for a while after we came back from Norway. But what I saw there (at the factory) were these incredibly exotic Mercedes-Benz cars.

Once I was offered a 300SL Gullwing, the old one that is now worth a fortune. We were going out on the road in the 1970s, and this guy heard I had a few cars, so they brought around two Gullwings, both in concours condition. Even back then, it seemed like just too much money. And I hemmed and hawed, and toward the end of rehearsals one had been sold, and he still had one. I was in that thing where you go like, "This is a *lot* of money." But I truly regret not buying that motorcar. The design was just phenomenal, and they remain phenomenal. The guy I bought my Porsche from in Maui has one in California. Seeing that car being brought back to life in this day and age is special. I have driven one, and it's a very expensive car, but if someone waved the magic wand, I would probably opt for one.

In marked contrast to the diminutive Austin 7, Mick's 2002 Porsche twin-turbo Carrera 4 resembles a stealth fighter plane. Low and wicked, black-on-black, it's an escape rocket for Fleetwood, despite his being limited by Maui's impossibly low speed limits. "I've found a few sneaky places where you can drive a car like the Porsche," he confesses.

robust designs of any motorcar I'd ever owned. It's spectacular, romantic, masculine, powerful, and I just thought the look of the car was extraordinary.

My friend Tony Nobles is a heart surgeon with an incredible car collection. He has a 275 GTB that's the same color, and very sweetly one night, we had dinner, and he said, "Would you like to take her out?" Of course I took Tony's car out for about an hour. Just moving off, I had a total flashback, and I got even sicker in my stomach that I ever got rid of it. I would love to own one of those again.

With English rock and rollers, the car connection was always about lifestyle, but there was also a sense of romance versus "Oh I want to look rich and famous." I think it was more poetic. Certainly with me, I used to buy cars that needed help. This whole episode of car love has to be treated as a romance. Musicians are romantic people.

But I do understand there are people who buy up cars as pure investment. When you go to Goodwood and you see people who run their cars, like Ralph Lauren—I've been around at meets and I don't know him, but I've seen him—he's connected to his cars. For someone who's gloriously wealthy, you can tell he's really looking at his cars as works of art.

That's well suited to musicianship. And that's the connection. People who are, quote, "artistic"— not that they are any wilder or better human beings than anyone else, don't get me wrong—I think they are suckers for romance. When you're in the arts, you are blessed because you are doing something that you love to do, and you've basically gotten lucky. So you hope to continue doing the thing you were romantically desirous of. . . .

The car gene exists in musicians, and that's why we're susceptible. Think of the poetry and the romance of hearing about driving through Italy with your lover. I identified with that notion, even when I had no money at all. I would go through hell; I would starve myself to make sure that my car that was burning oil, would have oil in it. So at any cost, I would have a decent pair of shoes, and I'd run an old car that was a total pain in the neck, but I loved it.

It was like having a dysfunctional lover.

There was a period in my life when I was blessed with having loads of money, and that's when I had a slew of motorcars. Then things calmed down, and I basically simplified my life. Now I have a souped-up 2002 twin-turbo 4WD Carrera Porsche. You don't really need fast cars in Hawaii, but I've found some sneaky places in the mountains where you can have fun in a car such as a Porsche. You can drive the hell out of it or treat it like a street car. I do both.

With English rock and rollers, the car connection was always about lifestyle, but there was also a sense of romance versus "Oh I want to look rich and famous." I think it was more poetic.

Clowning around a bit, Mick Fleetwood enjoys a morning drive in his little pet. Cheap and cheerful, the Austin 7 was considered Britain's Model T. These cars served many English families as reliable, affordable transport. Mick Fleetwood adores this car and plans never to sell it.

16

KEITH
URBAN

URBAN COWBOY

Many of the rockers you'll read about in this book love to drive fast. J Geils and Skid Row's Rachel Bolan have both raced on an amateur level, and AC/DC's frontman Brian Johnson made his professional racing debut at the 2011 Rolex 24 at Daytona International Speedway.

Keith Urban, on the other hand, likes to drive slowly. In fact, he compares driving slowly to riding around on a motorized couch.

"I think that must come from growing up with a dad who loved big '50s American cars," explains Urban, who today lives in Nashville, a world away from where he grew up.

Urban, forty-five, was born in New Zealand but grew up in Brisbane, Australia. "My dad grew up in the fifties and loved American culture, rock and roll, and cars. Ours was the only family in the neighborhood who always had an American car in the garage. We had Pontiacs and Chevys when nobody else in Australia had cars like that. He was part of an underground group of guys who loved these cars."

Couch cars or not, the Urbans were not opposed to mixing a bit of speed with their vehicle interests, and an annual family activity was a visit to the Bathurst 1000 races for Australian Touring Cars.

"It was a family institution," he says. "It was like our Super Bowl. I remember watching the drivers of that era, like Alan Moffat and Peter Brock, racing sedans on the track." But when it came time for Urban to purchase his own set of wheels,

Not many musicians can claim such an eclectic collection of automobiles. Urban drives all of his cars on a regular basis.

it wasn't one of his father's American dream cars or a wickedly fast Touring Sedan; it was, in fact, a truck. Like most rockers, hauling the band's equipment was more important than "hauling the mail."

Even when he moved to the United States in 1992 to expand his career as a country singer, he still found it necessary to own a truck. Shortly after arriving in Nashville, he bought a used 1985 Dodge Ram short-wheelbase van.

"I loved that thing," he remarks. "It had captain's chairs and just enough room for our equipment. It was like a Jeep on steroids."

There were advantages beyond cargo capacity in driving a van. One occasion, Urban and his drummer were driving the van to a studio for their first day of recording. It was a big day—one that he had dreamed of since childhood—as his band had just signed to record their first album.

It was about 9 a.m., and the musicians were stopped at a traffic light en route to the studio. Urban glanced into his rearview mirror, and a rapidly approaching truck seized his attention.

"I thought to myself, 'Boy, I hope that guy can stop. He's going pretty quick.' Just then, he slammed into the back of our van."

Urban jumped out of the van and went off on the truck's driver. After all, this was the biggest morning of his life, and they had almost bought the farm.

"I'm hurling insults at this guy," he recalls, "and my drummer got minor whiplash, but actually we got out fairly unscathed."

Now what to do? They had an appointment at the studio and no way to get there. Solution: Urban and his drummer squeezed into the front seat of the tow truck that had come to collect their van.

"The driver kindly dropped us off at the studio," he laughs. "When we got there, he had to pry the back doors open with a crowbar, and all our equipment fell out. As we loaded the guitars and drums into the studio, I turned around and waved bye-bye to the Dodge Ram, which I never saw again.

"That Ram gave its life to get us to the studio. I love that truck for doing that."

Talk about extremes! This behemoth 1956 Lincoln Mark II is one of Urban's favorites. The 5,000-pound car is a unique contrast to Urban's Fiat 500, which weighs half as much and takes up considerably less garage space.

CASH FOR CARS

In 1999, when his first $20,000 royalty check arrived, Urban could only think of one thing to spend it on: a car. Not a truck, but finally a car. And harking back to the large-car roots of his childhood, he had a particular model in mind.

"I wanted an Impala SS with the big 5.7-liter Corvette engine, which was built from 1992 to 1996," he says. "I found a black 1994 with only 3,500 miles on it in Charlotte, so I got a cheap flight to see the car.

"It was like the most rock-and-roll thing I had ever done: fly to test drive a car. I thought I had hit the big time."

Urban's plan was to talk the used car dealer down from the $23,000 asking price to $20,000, which was basically all the money he had at the time. But the car was perfect and even smelled new. He could find no faults.

"I had no negotiating power," he says. "None."

The dealer was intrigued, though, by Urban's story. Here was an up-and-coming Nashville artist buying a car from his little dealership! Sales promotion visions danced in his head.

"'Let me ask you a question, said the salesman. How much money do you charge for signing a bunch of autographs?'" My first thought was to tell him, 'None of your fucking business!', but I thought better of it," says Urban.

The salesman was angling for a way to offer this young musician the car for less money in return for a future autograph session.

"So I bought the Impala for $21,000 and drove it home," Urban says. "And I promised to return at some point in the future to sign a bunch of autographs."

Months rolled by, then years, but Urban never forgot his promise.

Four years later, Urban, who by that time had sold several million records, had a show in Charlotte.

Urban says his '56 Lincoln is the perfect car in which to practice the fine art of driving slow.

It was payback time. The dealer, who would have been satisfied with the up-and-coming status of the musician he'd met years earlier, had thousands of people crowding his dealership that day to see the now-popular country star.

"I showed up with my tour bus," says Urban. "It was a pretty crazy day."

As his fame grew, so did his car collection. He bought the ultimate "driving couch," a rare 1956 Lincoln Mk II.

"I'm a hardtop fan, not big on convertibles," he says. "It has more to do with the aesthetics and the line of the car. It's just my individual taste.

"When I drive this Lincoln, with its wonderful air-conditioning system, I can only imagine what it must have been like driving in 1956, when the only other place to stay cool was probably at the movies."

The black car with white interior is stunning, and he and his wife, actress Nicole Kidman—whom he calls "Nic"—love to take it cruising around the older, more-stately sections of Nashville.

"One day Nic and I were cruising at about thirty-five miles per hour in the Lincoln and she said to me, 'This is a great neighborhood. Have we been here before?' I said, 'Yeah, but we're usually flying through at seventy miles per hour with tinted windows, so we never really see it.'

"The Lincoln is a car we can just cruise in, talk, enjoy the landscape, and the actual act of driving."

Urban also owns a 1968 Lincoln, but to set the record straight, Urban is not only about motorized couches. For example, he owns a black resto-mod 1969 Mustang with a hopped up 351-cubic-inch engine, a custom leather steering wheel, and air-ride suspension. He

ABOVE: The Mustang's 351
V-8 features Shelby power
and dress-up accessories.

The tail of the snake, Urban's
wicked Shelby Mustang
clone. The resto-mod is
powered by a heavily
modified 351 Cleveland
engine and was a second-
anniversary present from his
wife, actress Nicole Kidman.

Urban stumbled across this original-condition, Astor Green 1968 Lincoln two-door hardtop while on tour in Pennsylvania. With a 462-cubic-inch V-8 under the hood, it runs beautifully.

discovered the car online but decided not to pursue it because he and his wife were expecting their first baby.

Nicole, though, impressed with the maturity brought on by her husband's impending fatherhood, surprised him by purchasing the hot Mustang. She wrapped the car with a big bow and presented it to him on their second wedding anniversary.

"I cried like a baby," he admits. "I told her, 'This stuff only happens to other guys.'"

These days, the Urban garage has an incredible assortment of thoroughbred cars from which to choose: a Rolls-Royce Ghost, a Porsche Cayenne, an Aston Martin Rapide, and interestingly, Fiat's tiny new 500, which he tows on tour in a trailer behind his motorcoach.

True to his country music roots, though, Urban sometimes just likes to cut loose and ride around Tennessee like a cowboy.

"I love driving my 1972 Chevy C-10 short-wheelbase pickup," he says. "It has a 350 engine with power for days. It only has an AM radio, so I tune it to a country station, crank up the volume, and just drive."

Motorized couch time . . . .

LEFT: The original, unrestored interior of Urban's 1968 Lincoln is in remarkable condition considering it's more than four decades old.

BELOW: Urban says the truck's light weight combined with a potent 350-cubic-inch engine makes it a great ride. "Initially I didn't like the color combination, but my wife saw it and loved it," he says

WHEN ROCKERS ROLL

When asked why so many rockers are also gearheads, Keith Urban was quite philosophical. "It's obvious the sexy guys went toward rock music and cars," he says, tongue-in-cheek. "It's a particular place, a very tribal place.

"To me, it just taps into all those things that are deeply tribal and masculine, like a warrior. It's bedded deep in our DNA of just wanting a stronger horse. I mean, what more does a guy really want than a great cave and a really strong horse? It all taps into the mythology of virility. It's all about peacocking.

"I'm sure there are infinitely deep, subconscious levels of why a guy like me likes certain things. But the strange part for me is that my tastes run the gamut all over the place—tiny cars, huge cars, cars that aren't about horsepower, and cars that are totally about horsepower."

Urban has a selection of motorcycles to choose from when he hits the road on tour, such as this beautiful, retro-styled Vengeance Drifter. He tows the bikes in a trailer behind the tour bus, sometimes accompanied by a new Fiat 500.

17

ARLO
GUTHRIE

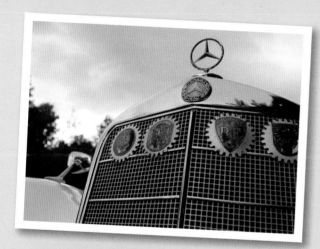

Guthrie is proud that all these original German grill medallions from driver's clubs and associations are still on the car. The previous owner was a Phil Hill of Los Angeles, though Guthrie is unsure whether it is the same Phil Hill that was America's first Formula 1 champion in 1961.

OPPOSITE: Guthrie struck this same pose for a Pioneer radio print ad he appeared in forty years ago. He bought this 1954 Mercedes-Benz 220 Cabriolet for $5,000 in 1970 while recording in Los Angeles. "Maybe someone reading your book would like to buy it," he says. Perhaps that would provide the funding to restore the Checker. . . .

A DIFFERENT TYPE OF COLLECTOR

The four-speed column shift in the vintage Mercedes-Benz is difficult to maneuver into gear. Even the most competent driver might need a lesson before venturing onto the road with the beautifully restored, ivory-colored classic. But as the car's forty-year caretaker, Arlo Guthrie has acquired a mechanical talent, and he easily slides the lever into and out of gear with amazing facility.

Guthrie has lived in the rural Berkshire Mountains of western Massachusetts since the mid-1960s. Because of his remote homestead, he developed a respect for all things mechanical. "When you live in the woods, you learn to tinker," says the sixty-four-year-old musician. "I'm not a real motor person, but I understand how they work. At least I can add enough duct tape to get it going again."

That skill came in handy during Guthrie's early concert-touring years. His Eagle-brand coach ran well going forward, but the transmission linkage wouldn't shift into reverse. "So I had to get my wife or someone else to sit up front and engage the clutch," says Guthrie. "Then I had to run around to the back of the bus and use a long metal pole to shove the linkage into gear. You become mechanically inclined even if you don't want to."

Today that Eagle tour bus sits silently in a field behind Guthrie's barn, joining four other coaches from Guthrie's touring career.

The Mercedes, a rare 1954 220A Cabriolet, has been part of Guthrie's life for more than four decades. His love affair with the car began on a sunny afternoon in 1970. He was recording a new album in Los Angeles, and because of the success of the *Alice's Restaurant* album, for the first time in his life, he had some cash.

"We came out to L.A. every year so I could work with some of the musicians I respected on the West Coast," explains Guthrie. "Guys like Ry Cooder. Typically we'd rent a house for three months, make some records, then go back home to the Berkshires."

One afternoon, soon after arriving in California, Guthrie was driving his rental car on Sunset Boulevard, near the intersection of the 405 Freeway, returning from a recording session, when his friend John Pilla's head snapped around.

"Arlo, look at that," Pilla said excitedly. "Look at that car."

Guthrie stopped his car to look at the vintage Mercedes. The asking price on the for-sale sign in the window read $5,000. He called the owner, took the car for a short test drive, and bought it on the spot.

The convertible ran flawlessly for the couple of months he used it in California, so when it was time to return to the East Coast, instead of flying, he and his wife Jackie, cradling their infant son Abe, climbed into the then sixteen-year-old car and drove it cross country.

"I loved the way it handled," he says. "It was the most balanced car I had ever driven. Well, except for my first car, the 1957 MGA I bought from Pete Seeger's son. That MG handled great, but I blew up three engines."

Guthrie's first automotive memories as a child were of his father, the late folk legend Woody Guthrie, driving Arlo, his brother, and sister in the family car during a snowstorm on the Belt Parkway in Brooklyn.

This 1954 Scenicruiser is becoming one with the earth in the field behind Guthrie's barn/office. The "Rising Son" emblazoned on the side is the name of Arlo's record label. He has had discussions with a motorcoach company in Florida that usually works on coaches for NASCAR drivers about the possibility of restoring the old tour bus to as-new condition.

"It was probably a 1938 Buick, or something like that," he says. "He had no interest in cars, or anything else of value for that matter.

"So the snow is flying and the car goes out of control on an elevated exit ramp. My brother and sister were terrified in the back seat, but my father laughed so hard. He thought it was funny and had no sense of danger. And I was freakin' thrilled and wanted to do it again. Somehow the car stayed on the road and didn't hit anything."

That automotive thrill ride has stayed with Guthrie ever since, both in cars and on motorcycles.

THE MOTORCYCLE SONG

As a young man, Guthrie would accompany his friends to sport car races at Lime Rock Park in Connecticut. Or he'd borrow a Triumph Bonneville and ride with friends to the scramble races in Millerton, New York.

Once he was riding the Triumph on a dirt track in Great Barrington. As he lapped faster and got more comfortable, he began leaning in the turns more and more, until the bike's foot peg became entangled in a tree root sticking out of the ground.

"That root wasn't moving, so, boom, I went right over," he recalls. "I was in a slight daze, but okay. But I started embellishing about the crash over the years in "The Motorcycle Song," with me going off cliffs and having all sorts of social significance.

"When you live in the woods, you learn to tinker. I'm not a real motor person, but I understand how they work. At least I can add enough duct tape to get it going again."

"I wrote that stupid song almost fifty years ago, but every night we perform, somebody will stand up and yell, 'Play "The Motorcycle Song,"' and it's usually some big Harley-looking guy with a big smile on his face."

Guthrie has one motorcycle these days, a 2001 Indian Centennial. "It's a special bike, and one of the last made in the original Springfield, Massachusetts, factory," says Guthrie. "It's not an authentic Indian in the sense that it doesn't have an Indian powerplant, but has an S&S motor. But it has that classic Indian styling."

Guthrie's favorite vehicle of all time? Ferrari? Rolls-Royce? Mercedes?

Nope.

Checker.

Checker?

"I can't think of a car that would be more fun right now than a brand-new Checker," he says.

Guthrie must be one of the few "civilians" to have owned not one, not two, but three Checkers. His first, purchased new in 1969, was a Manhattan Marathon model, which featured a longer wheelbase than the standard model.

"I ordered it new, and it was purple," says Guthrie. "I think I paid between $6,000 and $7,000 for the car. I could fit my whole band in that car—drum set, double bass, the guitars, and all the guys who played them. And we didn't even need to open the trunk. It was a tank. I loved it."

Over the years, the car rusted badly. But rather than junking it when he took it off the road, Guthrie instead recycled it. Since the engine still ran well, he converted the Checker's chassis and drivetrain into a saw mill, which he used to cut timber for use on his house, barn, and fences around his property.

Believe it or not, this fuel pump still operates. Guthrie has a tank filled with diesel fuel that he uses to fill his motorcoaches—those that are operable, that is.

"And I had the backseat converted into a couch that Jackie uses in her office," he says.

With the 1969 Checker's driving days over, Guthrie purchased another new Manhattan Marathon in 1982. But he never liked that car.

"It ran like shit," he says. "It was awful. No two screws were alike. It was the end of the Checker era, so they scrapped together the last few cars."

Three months after buying the Checker, he sold it and bought another 1969 model. Today, that car rests behind his barn but is slated for restoration.

So great was Guthrie's love for the classic-era Checkers that he considered purchasing the company when they ceased building cars.

"It was distinctive," he says. "I don't think they changed the design since 1955. They were tanks.

"I actually looked into buying the brand and converting them to propane or a hybrid electric power so they could be used as taxis in cities like New York just like English cabs are used in London.

"But I'm a folk singer, not a businessman, and I found out I didn't have enough money to buy the Checker company."

Besides, living in the woods of western Massachusetts, writing folk songs and fiddling with old cars and buses, suits Guthrie much more than being a high-powered auto executive.

Meet "Hanuman", a 1972 Eagle that was named after a Hindu monkey god. After serving fifteen years as Guthrie's home-on-the-road, it was sold to A. J. Croce, son of the late '70s singer/ songwriter Jim Croce. After three years, Croce was ready to trade up, so Guthrie bought it back. "It was our family's home for years," he explains.

ABOVE: Always story-telling, Guthrie talked for hours about his relationships with the various cars, motorcycles, and buses that have passed through his life. Even though he doesn't own a garage full of immaculate classics, his passion for all vehicles—cars, buses, and motorcycles—is obvious.

Guthrie's Mercedes is very complete, with the original owner's and service manuals still stored in the glove box.

The Mercedes features fabulous coachwork inside and out. The four-speed column shift takes some practice to master, but with four decades of practice, Guthrie is totally comfortable with its operation.

ANOTHER ALICE ADVENTURE

During the day we spent…, Arlo told photographer Michael Alan Ross and me about other automotive adventures during the day we spent with him at his house in the Berkshires. One of his stories sounded like another *Alice's Restaurant* episode.

"You remember Ray, don't you? He was Alice's husband. Well, I was getting ready to go on the road for a tour that would take most of the year. Ray needed a car, so I told him he could borrow my MGA while I was on the road. It was my pride and joy, and I told him to take care of it while I was gone because it was the best-handling car I had ever driven.

"When I got home months later, I went over to Ray's to pick up the car. 'I can't give it to you,' he said. 'I flipped it.'"

"'Flipped it? Ray, how did you flip it? It was the best handling car on the road.' When I asked him what he had done with it, he told me he made a saw mill out of the remains.

"I said, 'Ray, I need a car; I can't drive a saw mill!' So he gave me his best shotgun in trade. I didn't tell him that I couldn't drive a shotgun, so I just took it anyway.

"So I went home and hung the shotgun in my barn. The shotgun got stolen. Then I didn't have an MGA or a shotgun."

—Tom Cotter

ABOVE: All his grandkids are fighting over this car. Tired of his then-new 1983 diesel Cadillac Seville's constant breakdowns, he traded it even-up for this 12,000-mile 1966 Sedan Deville. "It was owned by a little old lady, a doctor's wife, who drove it to church on Sundays. It's never broken down," he says

Arlo needs a new lawn mower! Guthrie is a huge Checker fan. This 1969 Marathon was last registered in 1993, which came as something of a surprise to Guthrie. "No, it can't be that long!" he exclaims. He is waiting to win the lottery so he can afford to have it restored. "Someone reading this book may want to fix it for me. . . ."

18

PAT SIMMONS

Simmons' newest bike is this 1990 Harley-Davidson FLHS, which is his daily rider. Though Hawaii is beautiful, he misses the seemingly endless number of perfect motorcycle roads in Northern California.

DOOBIE BROTHERS
ROCKIN' DOWN THE HIGHWAY

As Pat Simmons discovered, if you are a fan of old motorcycles, life on the road is not too bad.

The founding member, guitarist, and vocalist of the Doobie Brothers has spent four decades on the road crooning classics like "China Grove," "Jesus Is Just Alright," and "Takin' It to the Streets." And much of the time, he never steps on his tour bus without a copy of *Hemming's Motor News*.

Life on the road and in hotel rooms can be boring, so he opens up *Hemming's* or buys the local newspaper and looks for old motorcycles in the classifieds.

"I went around the country and bought a lot of bikes," he says. "I was the original Picker! I was always looking for [Harley-Davidson] Panheads and Shovelheads. And I was buying 1940s Indians too."

Like many of his generation, the teenage Simmons had two loves: rock and roll and motorcycles. On the music front, the sixteen year old was learning to play guitar and jamming with a couple of high-school bands. He also worked after school in a gas station. When his dad's 1953 Chevy needed an engine overhaul, Simmons tackled the rebuild under the watchful eye of the station's mechanic.

"I reground the valves, installed new rings on the pistons, and honed the cylinders," he says. "I cut my teeth on seeing the inside of an engine. That was the start for me."

A few years later, he was offered a free BSA 441 Victor. All he had to do was pick it up in northern California. He had driven up with a friend, hoping to ride the

One of the benefits to building a new shop at his Hawaii home was that Simmons was able to put everything in one location. "It's the first time in the last twenty years that I've had a shop where I can actually put everything and have room to work on the bikes," explains Simmons.

bike home, but when he arrived, he discovered it was completely disassembled. So he loaded boxes of parts, the frame, and the engine into his MGBGT hatchback and hauled it home.

Back home in San Jose, he bought a BSA repair manual and, armed with little more than a pair of pliers, a Vise-Grip, and a screwdriver, he had that bike on the road within two weeks.

At about the same time, Simmons' music career began to take off. Teaming up with fellow guitarist and singer Tommy Johnston, drummer John Hartman, and bass player Dave Shogren, they formed a band called the Doobie Brothers in 1970.

The Doobie Brothers drew an audience of motorcyclists in the San Francisco Bay area who would show up at bars to hear the band perform. As their

popularity grew, they picked up a reputation as a "biker band," especially when the Hells Angels turned out en masse whenever the band played at the Chateau Liberté in the Santa Cruz Mountains.

"We all dressed in leather jackets and leather pants, and we had this tough-guy image," says Simmons. "I'd ride up to the shows on my BSA, and Tommy had his Norton. We lived the image."

Simmons' interest in bikes, especially old bikes, became a passion. He and a friend opened Classic Motorcycles of Santa Cruz, which specialized in parts and bolt-on accessories for vintage Harley-Davidson and Indian motorcycles. To dress up the showroom and attract customers, Simmons began to buy and display vintage bikes. He got a tip from a friend that an older gentleman in northern California had some old bikes for sale.

"He had four Harleys: a 1917, a 1922, a 1925, and a 1929," says Simmons. "I thought the price was way too high—$2,000 for all four—but I bought them anyway."

Simmons also bought a few motorcycles from Bud Ekins, a legend in the motorcycle world and frequent stunt double for movie star Steve McQueen. Ekins' Hollywood-area warehouse was famous among collectors. Simmons said Ekins stored bikes on double-stacked racks around the inside perimeter of his building.

"He probably had 300 bikes, and everything was pre-1916," he says.

Every time Simmons visited Ekins, he learned something. Or bought something.

"If I bought a bike from Bud for $5,000, I'd sell it for $5,200 and feel great about a $200 profit," says

Simmons. "At least it would pay the light bill at the shop."

In 1982, Simmons closed his shop. Even though he loved the business, he was on the road more and more. Plus, his partner was losing interest. That didn't stop him from hunting for old bikes.

He worked out quite a racket. Whether riding in his tour bus or hanging around his hotel room while on tour, he spent his free time looking for old bikes to buy. When he scored, he would stow his purchases inside the Doobie Brothers' equipment tractor-trailer truck, thus delivering the bikes back to California at the tour's conclusion.

One of his more memorable finds was in Michigan, where a widow was advertising her deceased husband's 1941 Indian 4.

The oldest bike in Simmons' collection is this 1904 Indian with the camelback gas tank over the rear wheel. He acquired it in this condition in 1983 and plans to restore it in the near future.

"He had been restoring it before he died," recalls Simmons. "So she gave me the price, and I agreed to buy it. Then the woman's daughter asked if I might be interested in a second bike."

Simmons didn't even know there was another bike and looked under the tarp in the garage to find another Indian.

"It was a 1947 Chief with an oddball metalflake brown paint scheme," he says. "This one had a sidecar with all these sprockets and chains hooked up to the handlebars.

"It turns out the woman's son was paraplegic and couldn't walk, so her husband converted the bike so it could be operated with just his hands."

He bought the unusual Chief as well.

In the late 1980s, Simmons met an intriguing woman when the Doobie Brothers were performing a charity concert for muscular dystrophy in conjunction with the Sturgis Motorcycle Rally in South Dakota. Cris Sommer was a journalist and author, covering the event for *Harley Women*, a magazine she owned. The two were introduced by Harley-Davidson executive Clyde Fessler and they spent the evening walking around Sturgis, talking motorcycles.

Everywhere you look in Simmons' shop, you see fascinating parts and memorabilia. When working on your own bikes, especially rare antiques, an extensive literature and reference collection is indispensable.

Sommer and Simmons married, and not surprisingly, their motorcycle collection grew.

Today, the couple lives in Hawaii and owns about forty motorcycles, most of them American antiques. The newest bikes in their stable are Simmons' 1990 Harley FLHS and Sommer-Simmon's 1988 Heritage.

Some of the bikes in their collection include a 1901 Columbia, a 1905 Indian, a 1910 Indian single, a 1911 Indian belt drive, a 1912 Harley (which Steven Wright had restored for Steve McQueen), a 1913 Thor (which finished third in the Del Mar Concours), a 1913 Excelsior, a 1914 Indian four-valve racer, and a 1916 Indian Powerplus with original paint.

Learning how to rebuild his father's Chevy engine all those years ago has paid Simmons back in spades. Today, he and Cris perform all their own mechanical work.

"I'm not afraid to pull apart and rebuild a motor. They are not that complicated."

The couple's mechanical talents were put to the test in 2011. Sommer-Simmons decided to enter the cross-country Cannonball Rally, a 3,000-mile ride open only to motorcycles built prior to 1916, that started in Kitty Hawk, North Carolina, and ended in San Francisco.

ABOVE: Because of his lifelong interest in motorcycles and his classic rocker looks, Pat Simmons considers himself "the last Doobie Brother." The reward for his long, successful career is a handsome Maui home and shop that he shares with his motorcycle-riding wife, author Cris Sommer-Simmons. BELOW LEFT: Simmons' two passions, music and riding, both find homes in his garage space. He got this 1920s-era Gibson as payback some 30 years ago from a fellow who owed him money after Simmons bailed him out of jail. BELOW RIGHT: Simmons' memorabilia collection extends to tin and diecast motorcycle toys as well.

This restored 1912 Harley-Davidson single came from another serious collector of American motorcycles, the late actor Steve McQueen.

Simmons had owned a 1915 Harley for decades, but it had spent that time sitting in a California barn. He dusted off the bike and began prepping it for the rally. With less than ten test miles on the bike, Sommer-Simmons mounted the bike and rode it among forty-four other bikes for sixteen days, averaging forty-three miles per hour.

After his concert tour was over, Simmons joined his wife's pit crew in a team van that shadowed the tour across the United States.

"It was the ride of my life," says Sommer-Simmons, who wrote a book about the experience. "But I'm not going to do that again…"

Simmons' favorite bike from his collection is the same 1915 Harley that his wife rode cross country. It was recently on display at the Harley-Davidson Museum in Milwaukee.

"After all these years, I'm like the last bike guy standing," says Simmons. "I'm the last guy in the band who still rides. I'm the last Doobie Brother."

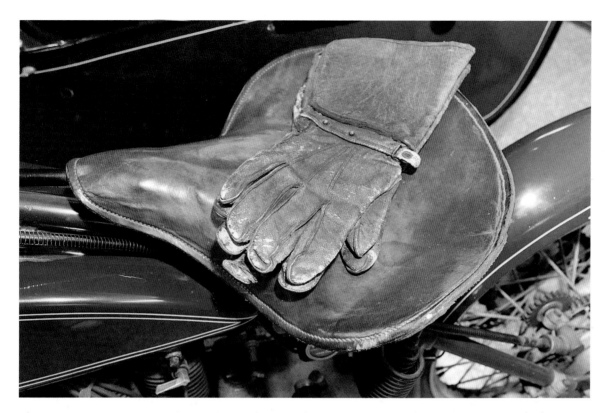

LEFT: These period riding gloves rest on the seat of a sidecar-equipped 1920 Ace. The Ace was once part of Steve McQueen's extensive collection of antique motorcycles.

BELOW: Simmons' 1912 Harley-Davidson X8A single once belonged to movie star and antique-bike collector Steve McQueen. The photo perched atop the fork shows McQueen starting the bike.

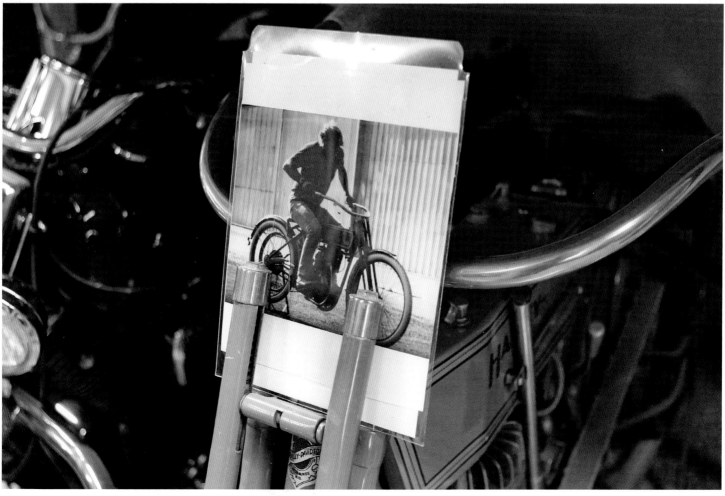

A terrific old barn-find and one of the gems in the Simmons collection is this original-paint 1916 Indian Powerplus v-twin.

Quite the vintage line-up both musically and two wheeled. Bikes from left to right: 1965 Harley-Davidson Panhead, 1941 Indian 4, 1916 Indian Powerplus. Guitars from left to right, back row: 1964 Gibson SG Special, 1940s Gibson L-7, 1966 Epiphone Texan (Simmons got this when he was sixteen or seventeen, wrote the hit "Black Water" on it, and has played it on every Doobie Brothers record), 1934 National resonator guitar, 1970 custom-paint Gibson 335, 1920s Gibson. In the front row at left is a 1956 Gretsch 6120.

PHOTOGRAPHER'S NOTES

When Tom Cotter asked if I'd be interested in doing the photography for this book, my heart skipped a beat. It had nothing to do with any sort of celebrity, star-struck fantasies or visions of becoming the next "in demand" shooter for the music business. Instead, it had everything to do with the fact that this project is who I am—and Tom didn't even know it.

I became a full-time musician right out of high school and played in thousands of smoky bars, sang on jingles, and didn't own a suit or a tie. Just like several of the artists featured in this book, my first vehicle was all about hauling my musical equipment. But like the musicians in this book, I am a gearhead and I couldn't just leave my hauler stock. So, there I was at midnight, lying in the driveway in my black leather jacket with nothing more than a mechanic's trouble light and a ball-peen hammer trying to line up my headers with those flat black Hooker side pipes. The vehicle? A Dodge Tradesman 100 van. It was Top Banana Yellow with black stripes, the aforementioned side-pipes, trick wheels and tires, oversized sway bars, fog lamps and aircraft landing lamps mounted in the front bush bar. It hauled my equipment, and it hauled ass!

Over the years I swapped my guitars and amps for cameras and tripods, and the smoky venues gave way to racetracks and beautiful backdrops. But I'm still hauling equipment, drivin' hard, creating, and blasting the music!

Each and every musician I had the pleasure of photographing for this book approaches life with passion and an appreciation for creativity. They understand the process and the hard work that goes into being a success. Their passion for both music and cars and motorcycles and their admiration of design makes perfect sense to me. It's creativity and math all crammed into the same brain—a perfect merging of the left side with the right. A melody is either memorable or not, just like the curve of a fender, a handlebar, or an instrument. Time is the true test of both music and design. When it's right, it's right.

This was a wonderful experience for me. Sure, now I can name drop with the best of them, but no one can take these memories away from me. Riding shoulder to shoulder with Brian Johnson in his 1928 Bentley Le Mans, listening to Arlo Guthrie tell stories about getting speeding tickets, and sitting in Austin with Jimmie Vaughan eating real Texas barbeque. Hell, I was harnessed into the back of Tom Cotter's Mini Cooper shooting Brian

Johnson's Lola at Road Atlanta while the crowd sat and wondered "who the heck is that maniac? Lucky bastard!" After years of singing "New York State of Mind", there I was, suddenly directing "The Piano Man" on where to stand by the old train station in Oyster Bay and asking him to give me that Cheshire cat grin once again.

I've played not one, but two of Wayne Henderson's guitars, tore through the curves with J Geils in a Lancia and later with Jol Dantzig in a lightweight '73 Porsche 911 RS. I even went out on a limb and suggested photographing John Oates in front of an abandoned luncheonette (get it?).

With each and every musician, it was an instant connection. I'd like to thank them all for the respect they extended me through the creative process to get the shots seen throughout this book.

We have the automobile and the motorcycle to thank for this. Our favorite forms of transportation are what connect us all. I've seen it on the lawns of Pebble Beach, on the streets of Sturgis, in back alley garages and at the Cite de l'Automobile. These rolling sculptures are our common language, just like music.

—Michael Alan Ross
Photographer

INDEX